I Met a Miracle

The story of my own encounter
with the claims of Christ
and other remarkable stories

George E. Vandeman

Pacific Press® Publishing Association
Nampa, Idaho
Oshawa, Ontario, Canada
www.pacificpress.com

ISBN 978-0-8163-4012-5

Cover design by Steve Lanto.

Originally published in 1971.

The author assumes full responsibility for the accuracy of all facts and quotations as cited in this book.
In addition to the King James Version, the following versions have been quoted:

The New Testament in Modern English, revised edition, copyright 1958, 1959, 1960, 1972 by J. B. Phillips. Published by the Macmillan Company and Collins Publishers.
The New English Bible, copyright by the Delegates of the Oxford University Press and the Syndics of the Cambridge University Press 1961 and 1970.
The Bible: A New Translation by James Moffatt. Copyright, 1954. Used by permission of Harper and Row, Publishers, Inc.

Heritage Project
This book is part of the Pacific Press® Heritage Project, a plan to re-publish classic books from our historical archives and to make valuable books available once more. The content of this book is presented as it was originally published and should be read with its original publication date in mind.
You can obtain additional copies of this book by calling toll-free 1-800-765-6955 or by visiting www.adventistbookcenter.com. You can purchase this as an e-book by visiting www.adventist-ebooks.com.

ISBN: 978-0-8163-4012-5   0-8163-4012-9

Table of Contents

Introduction

I love personal stories. I love testimonies. I love hearing about how an encounter with God changes people—how it transforms their lives. Perhaps my all-time favorite is this story—the story of my father's turning point—his conversion.

I can still remember sitting in evangelistic meetings as a child, listening to my dad tell about the Friday night he shook his fist at the heavens and said "Holy Spirit, leave me and never come back!"

That Friday night was his crossroads moment—his turning point. *I Met a Miracle* was first published more than fifty years ago, but the story of how an encounter with Jesus changed one man's life—and through him many other lives—is timeless.

In the pages of this book you'll read the story of how my precious dad, George E. Vandeman was changed through meeting Jesus. As you read, I hope that you, too, will have an encounter with the Saviour. May every turning point in *your* life lead you to Jesus!

Connie Vandeman Jeffery
Associate Speaker—*Voice of Prophecy*
October 2012

Chapter 1

I Met a Miracle

It was on a Friday night that I shook my fist at God.

Five minutes before it happened you would have written me down as a decent, respectable, promising young man with drive and dedication and—well, going somewhere. But inside I was riot and revolt and rebellion and civil war and guilt—all rolled into a bored, frustrated kid, generation gap and all.

I kept my distance from anyone over thirty. In fact, I wanted little to do with anyone or anything that reminded me of my early background.

My father was a minister. I don't mean the kind of minister who marches in parades and preaches politics and goes to jail for causes he believes in. Not that he would not gladly have followed his conscience to prison if there had been a need. But things were different in those days. Concern for people was not concentrated in the streets.

But my father understood men. He helped men. He won men. And I watched and listened and was deeply impressed. I learned even before my teens that sermons do not come from mental discipline and wide reading and scholastic achievement alone—however essential these may be—but from life.

There wasn't a trace of phoniness in my father, or in my family, or in my home church, as far as I can remember. That was one problem I did not have. Rather than being turned away from religion by people who didn't live it, I was constantly being drawn back to it by the compelling demonstration of God's power to change lives—drawn back, I say, while I was trying desperately to escape.

You see, I had this hang-up about freedom. I didn't want to be restricted. I didn't want to be fenced in. I didn't want to be inhibited. I wanted to make up my own rules. And as a minister's son, I was being watched. And I didn't want to be watched.

It was more than that. Early in my teens, gnawing away at my restless mind, came the first faint suggestions that God might someday call me into the ministry. I confess that the idea surprised me. And it was to surprise those who knew me even more.

These were convictions I was determined to stifle. For however appealing my home background, and however insistent the call of God to my young heart, I determined to stifle the inner voice and discover life for myself.

I hadn't heard about the evils of the establishment in those days. So I would be wise, I thought. I would safeguard my future security by preparing to be a civil engineer. I'm not sure whether I really wanted to be a civil engineer, or whether I just didn't want to be a minister. I knew, of course, that if God wants a man to go to Nineveh—wherever that Nineveh may be—no other place will do. And, besides, I had a lurking suspicion that the thing I was fighting was the thing I really wanted. I was all mixed up, and unwilling to admit it to anyone, much less to myself.

I tremble to think of what I so narrowly escaped. No, there were no brushes with the law. There was nothing in my conduct revolting to society or even embarrassing to my family. No scandals to live down.

I know now that conversion is easier for a man whose sins are etched in deep scarlet. Such a man, unless he has completely silenced the voice of God to his heart, knows where he stands. He knows he needs God.

But I was gripped by something worse. Mine were respectable sins. I was lost in the church. And don't let anybody tell you it can't happen. Because it can. Please believe me. It is altogether possible to accept a theory, to be satisfied with a form of religion, and yet be lost—lost in the church.

Oh, I would go to church and hear a sermon, and I would be concerned. I would read the newspaper and see events following Bible prediction like a blueprint, and I would be troubled. But when I tackled my own natural weaknesses— and sometimes I did want to tackle them—I was completely helpless.

I think that was the real problem. Religion, at least my experience with it, seemed to be very weak on the how. And of what use is a religion that doesn't work?

And so I rebelled. What else was there to do? I took up with every respectable symbol of rebellion. Long hair and beads and guitar it would have been, if it had happened today. Of course a guitar, for instance, doesn't necessarily mean rebellion. My daughter Connie plays one—and I love it. But for some—a symbol. I took up with those who were "in" at the time. I'm thankful that chemical rebellion wasn't popular.

I became so weary of boredom and defeat that I tried to run away from conscience. But, thank God, conscience—unless you kill it—will never let you go.

God did not leave me alone, though I wanted to be left alone. Like a man who has taken too many sleeping pills, I needed to be walked and walked and walked. And God was right there. And it made me uncomfortable. I didn't want Him that close.

I felt like global war inside. And the war was not de-escalating.

Finally I could stand it no longer. It was a Friday evening, and I was seated in a meeting where my father was speaking. There he stood—my ideal of a minister, my ideal of a man.

He was speaking to the entire congregation, not to me in particular. But every word he said cut like a knife. I got up and walked out of the meeting and moved restlessly into the shadows. I shall never forget those moments. In that still summer evening, looking up past the trees into God's own sky, I actually shook my fist at the heavens and said, "Holy Spirit, leave me! And don't ever come back!"

Thank God, that prayer was never answered! But breathing those words, the shock of having said them, did something to me. At least the words were prayer, though bitter in their defiance.

This was the climax to a long series of events in which the evil one had been overstepping himself. I had been doing things that surprised even myself. And now, by my own defiant words, I was thoroughly shocked. For the first time I saw the fine print on the devil's contract. And I decided to break it.

Little did I dream that I was standing on the threshold of a transforming experience that would dwarf all my former visions of personal happiness and satisfaction. I was to learn a secret that would not only change my own restless soul, but would do the same for any man who is secretly longing to know.

And that is what I want to share with you in these pages. Not just my own story. Rather, growing out of it, building upon its discoveries, focusing from many angles, I want to introduce you to my Lord. I want to talk with you about some of the questions that so perplexed and confused and haunted me—until I found the way out. I want to do this because I know that the questions that tapped so insistently at my mind must have tapped at your mind, too. For really we are all alike. The problems don't change with generations—only the vocabulary, only the scene.

Is there such a thing as peace of mind? Is there any cure for guilt? Are prayers ever answered? Can God really change a man? How does He do it? What sort of commitment is required? And how deep is a man's involvement? What risk does he take?

The questions are not profound. Neither are the answers. You will not need any theological background to understand this book. And if you have picked it up expecting to find entertainment, or involved philosophy, or unique literary beauty, you will be disappointed. This is a book for the man in need, the man confused, the man defeated, the man at the end of his rope. A man who is sinking doesn't want oratory. He wants a lifeline. And that is what this book is about.

But back to my story. For many months the secret I was seeking seemed to evade me. I set out at once to reconstruct my life, to set my house in order, to realign my thinking and my goals. I knew what was right. But religion, I say, seemed to be weak on the *how*. *Information* was not enough. I needed *demonstration*—in my own life.

What worried me was that no matter how vigorous were my attempts at self-improvement, I repeatedly failed. Yet strangely enough, when I asked older Christians how to succeed in my personal life, how to break the power of wrong habit, their counsel was simply, "Try harder."

Listen. If anyone tells you to try harder, tell him he is wrong! I know, they may not call it *trying*. They may call it self-discipline. They may offer you some psychological formula, some new secret for tapping a power they say is within you, even some very worthy involvement in the needs of society. But is it not the same old *trying*—trying to lift yourself by your own power? It doesn't work. You can try until you are weary. You can try until you are worn out. But still your weaknesses will mock you. Trying only focuses attention upon yourself. It is a power outside yourself, the power of the living God, that changes and transforms. The only way to get into the kingdom of God is to be born into it—by a miracle. It is just that simple. But I didn't understand.

And so, although it sounded a little too much like self-hypnosis, I whipped up my determination again, flexed my muscles, and made another try. But before long my willpower relaxed, and I found myself right back where I started. This resulted in discouragement. And if there was anything I did not need, it was discouragement. Or did I? At least it jarred me into action.

Evidently something was wrong here—something terribly wrong. I dropped to my knees. I opened the Bible. For if this business of Christian living was genuine, there would have to be a more adequate demonstration of it in my life. Certainly there ought to be more to the gospel than another chance after every defeat.

Now came the surprise. As I opened the Scriptures, I found no emphasis on self-discipline. Instead, I found such words as these: "Can the Ethiopian change his skin, or the leopard his spots? then may ye also do good, that are accustomed to do evil." Jeremiah 13:23. And the words of Jesus: "Do men gather grapes of thorns, or figs of thistles? . . . Neither can a corrupt tree bring forth good fruit." Matthew 7:16-18.

No wonder it could not be done by rigid mental effort! No wonder all my noble resolutions were about as strong as ropes of sand!

And then imagine how I felt as I discovered in the seventh chapter of Romans a description of the very conflict I was experiencing like a broken record. Listen to Paul's words, beginning with verse 15, as Dr. J. B. Phillips has translated them: "My own behavior baffles me. For I find myself not doing what I really want to do but doing what I really loathe. . . . My conscious mind wholeheartedly endorses the Law, yet I observe an entirely different principle at work in my nature. . . . In my mind I am God's willing servant, but in my own nature I am bound fast, as I say, to the law of sin and death. It is an agonizing situation, and who on earth can set me free from the clutches of my own sinful nature? I thank God there is a way out through Jesus Christ our Lord."

A way out! That brought courage. Evidently the difficulty was in my own sinful nature. I began to understand why it is that a man sins. I realized that this planet is in rebellion against a good and loving God, and that a fallen, corrupt, degenerate nature has been passed on from generation to generation, that sin and disobedience and rebellion have so warped and undermined the perfect nature with which God originally endowed man that it is utterly impossible for any man, in his own strength, to live for God.

No wonder I had made so little progress in solving my problems. How could it be otherwise, so long as my fundamental nature was unchanged? I had attempted to cover conflict and defeat by outward discipline. I had been content to keep my objectionable traits of character, while I grasped frantically for grace and poise and personality to cover them up. But I was missing the real point.

How often I had seen it in others! For it is one thing for a hostess to keep sweet and charming at a social function when a guest soils her lovely gown—outwardly calm while she is burning inside. It is one thing for an employer to be courteous to a bungling workman, a blundering customer, when influence and reputation are at stake—though all the while hate burns in his heart. But it is quite another thing to have a power inside that will take away the hate and the burning.

I saw that patching up the outside could never heal the inside. I could not cover defeat with culture, or weakness with personality. I must have a power that could go deeper than that, or forever live with a mocking heart.

But light began to dawn. Hope sprang up as I read such words as are found in 1 Thessalonians 5:24: "Faithful is he that calleth you, *who also will do it.*" He promises to do it. And I had been trying to do it myself.

And then I read Jude 24: "Now unto him that is *able to keep you from falling,* and to present you faultless." Here was not partial victory—the kind I was experiencing.

And 2 Peter 1:4 solved the problem: "Whereby are given unto us exceeding great and precious promises: that by these ye might be *partakers of the divine nature.*"

I saw now why simply working at it had proved so disappointing. Evidently God had planned to do something deep and fundamental within me, and I had not permitted it. It was a new nature that I needed.

A friend helped me one day with a very simple illustration. Let us suppose, he suggested, that a timber wolf should watch and admire the habits of a flock of peaceful sheep and decide that that is the way an animal ought to live. Suppose he attempts now to live just as a sheep lives. Would not that wolf have a difficult time? Would he not be likely to slip back to his old way of life? Grass might seem quite tasteless as he remembered feeding on some carcass.

But suppose that God by a miracle known only to the Creator should transplant into the wolf the nature of a sheep. Then would it be difficult to live like a sheep? Not at all.

Well, it helped me. The possibility described in 2 Corinthians 5:17 now made sense. How had I missed the very thing I needed? Listen: "Therefore if any man be in Christ, he is a new creature: old things are passed away; behold, all things are become new."

I stood in wonder before the utter simplicity of God's plan. How could it have been so difficult to grasp? Did it need to be? Would a God so anxious to save us reveal the way in words we could not understand? Surely not.

Unfortunately, the language of religion, its familiar vocabulary, like the repetitious chiming of a bell, sometimes just doesn't register. We hear the words so often that we scarcely hear them at all. How many times my father had tried to tell me the secret! But I never got the message.

It was amazing how all the Scripture statements on this subject now seemed to fall into place, as in an almost-completed puzzle. The incident related in John 3 became more vital to me than I had ever dreamed possible. You will remember that Nicodemus—a man thoroughly respected, highly trained, possessed of a dignity and culture rarely seen in those times— came to Jesus by night. And there under a Middle Eastern sky the Saviour of men kindly but forcefully probed to the heart of his problem as He said, "Except a man be born again, he cannot see the kingdom of God."

Strong words, these. And Nicodemus did not understand. He questioned the possibility of rebirth. But Jesus pressed home His point again: "Except a man be born of water and of the Spirit, he cannot enter into the kingdom of God."

My wonder deepened at these words of Jesus. Evidently such a transformation is possible. But how could it be brought about? God did not leave me without an answer—one that had been there all the time: "Which were born, not of blood, nor of the will of the flesh, nor of the will of man, but of God." John 1:13.

The new birth was not something that could come about through *the will of man.* No wonder I had failed!

True, I had changed direction. I had decided to break my contract with rebellion. I had faced the unpleasant task of confession. I had felt the remorse that Peter must have felt when he betrayed and denied his Lord. I had come to the place where I could say, "I am sorry. No one else is responsible. I am to blame. God help me!"

All this was opening the floodgates for the change I needed—the new birth. But nothing I could do could bring it about.

Unquestionably I was facing a miracle. And did I, George Vandeman, master of my own future—did I have to submit to a miracle? Evidently. For the man who is attempting to remake himself without God is attempting an impossibility. The Christian life is not simply a modification or an improvement of the old. Rather, it is a transformation of a man's nature that for all practical purposes recreates him. He is a new man. Since the day I discovered that secret, my deepest satisfaction has been on seeing the new light in the eyes of men and women as this truth dawns.

It all came about so effortlessly. And I had tried so hard! Listen: "No one sees the hand that lifts the burden, or beholds the light descend from the courts above. The blessing comes when by faith the soul surrenders itself to God. Then that power which no human eye can see creates a new being in the image of God."—Ellen G. White, *The Desire of Ages,* p. 173.

No one sees the hand. But the miracle is there!

Tongue cannot tell it. Pen cannot write it—the peace this transaction brings to the human breast. This is the transforming secret that was to dwarf every youthful dream into insignificance. I learned it the hard way. But I learned it never to forget!

Let me take you back to that night when I stood in the shadows, looking up at the stars. Had I been examined that night on the theory of truth, I would have passed with flying colors. In fact, if my father had been called away by some emergency, I think I could have preached his sermon at least with clarity. But it was not theory I needed—or clarity. *It was life!*

I knew then and there that if ever these lips or this pen were commissioned to share truth with others, power must attend it or it would accomplish nothing. I knew even that night the terrible responsibility of the ministry. For no man or woman is ever the same after he has confronted the claims of Christ.

I knew then, as I know much better now, that it is possible for men with eternal destinies at stake to accept a theory of truth and yet lose out. For without the transforming process that comes alone through divine power, the original tendencies to sin are left in the heart in all their strength, there to forge new chains and impose a slavery that the power of man can never break!

I had so narrowly escaped such a slavery that I determined no one within the hearing of my voice would ever step back into life unaware of its danger. God help the man who rests passively and unafraid under the shadow of a superficial profession, an outward cloak of religion! He is the man I sincerely pray my ministry may help.

I realize now that the struggle of that night under the stars was in reality the beginning of my ministry—and the reason for it. God knew that the real desire of that lonely heart was just the opposite of the words that escaped those lips. The desperate cry of the soul—that His Spirit might *never* leave—is the prayer He heard that night. And forever I thank God!

Chapter 2

Prices People Pay

There is no limit to the price a man will pay for peace of mind!

You see him washing in the sacred Ganges. Walking through a bed of flame. Making a pilgrimage to Mecca. Marking the stations along Jerusalem's Way of the Cross.

Closer home, you see him meditating, marching, hallucinating. Spending a year in the Peace Corps. Tutoring a ghetto student. Writing checks to charity. Protesting war. Or visiting a psychiatrist. Trying to hitchhike his way to inner peace.

But can peace of mind, this inner peace, be bought with penance or with prayers? Can it be purchased with sacrifice or fasting? Can it be earned by involvement in our deepening social problems? Can the mind be disciplined or meditated or hallucinated into happiness?

Why the modern trek to the East? Will man find in ancient lore the answer to his spiritual longings?

Peace of mind! Why is it so elusive? Never has man sought it in such frantic desperation. And the path to attain it, cut deep by the disappointments of the centuries, has never been more forbiddingly difficult—or more delightfully simple!

It is no wonder that men and women are frustrated in their search. For modern man treads a narrow trail that barely skirts destruction. His emotional conflicts, his economic insecurities, overwhelm him. He is afraid.

People are afraid. And so they look about for devices, for techniques of salvation, for some restorer of inner equilibrium, some shock-proof balance that will enable them to walk the tightrope of this mad century safely.

But peace of mind is not something that can be bought in bottles, or applied like a cosmetic, or obtained by taking a capsule before meals or enrolling in a course for three evenings a week. It is not the doped-up bliss of Aldous Huxley's *Brave New World.* No!

Peace of mind? Quite an undertaking. The centuries have proved it.

Back of the splash of color and ritual in the Eastern lands is persistent evidence of this universal search. Again and again I have witnessed it.

Watch in the courtyard of the fire-walking temple of Singapore as the pit of flame is prepared and tended through the day. There is the heavy odor of burning incense, the pulsating rhythm of the drums, the parading of gaudy idols.

And then the fire walkers are ready. Excited into a trance, they run through the flame, bathing their feet in a pool of goat's milk at the end of the pit. If one falters in the fire, he is lashed with a whip and hurried on.

It makes you feel like climbing to the top of the temple and shouting, "You don't have to do this! There is a better way!"

But that is the heart, the central concept, of Eastern religions. The Hindus of India, trying to bathe or burn away their sins. The Buddhists with their yellow-robed monks and disciplined meditation. The followers of Confucius, hiding frustration with festival.

There is the world of Islam, with its submission. What must the Muslim *do?* Five things. He must publicly confess his faith, he must pray five times daily, he must give alms, he must fast during the entire month of Ramadan, and he must make a pilgrimage to Mecca at least once during his lifetime.

Yes, trying to earn tomorrow with today. Trying to persuade some distant, unconcerned deity to look your way and not be too hard on you. Buying salvation with Brownie points. Has some of it rubbed off on us?

"What must I *do* to be saved?" is the heart cry of the centuries. "What must I *do?* How can I attain peace of mind?"

And echoing back from the lips of still-bewildered millions comes the answer, "Earn it. Deserve it. Buy it. Do penance. Atone. *Work, work, work!*"

But that isn't God's answer. God said through the Apostle Paul that night in the Philippian jail, "Believe on the Lord Jesus Christ, and thou shalt be saved." Acts 16:31.

Christianity, then, is different. I wish that we always remembered it. I wish that we always understood.

How pathetic it is to be mistaken about what constitutes true worship! What strange duties men assume, what strange altars they build, in their search for peace of mind! Do they find it? Tranquility of a sort, perhaps. But it isn't the kind of peace that God gives. Jesus said, "Peace I leave with you, my peace I give unto you: not as the world giveth, give I unto you." John 14:27.

What is peace of mind—God's kind? What is it that man, down through the centuries, has desired so deeply that he is willing to pay any price, build any altar, do any penance, make any sacrifice, to obtain it? Is it only an elusive myth? An impossible dream?

Behind the mask of involvement, the camouflage of concern, the whirl of commitment, the oratory of protest, there is a crescendo of frustration that cannot be missed. From the battered pavement of Main Street to the comfortable niches of suburbia to the desks of megalopolis it is the same. What is it that man really wants? What does God hear as He listens to the beat of the heart?

Said a college student, "I am . . . blue and lonesome all at once, standing by the dance floor trying to look fearless and suave, while inside I feel like running somewhere to cry."

Yes, many a student is toying with clinical psychology with the hope that hidden away in the jargon of thick books, behind the mask of mastering therapy for others, he might figure out himself. He hopes in the process to find peace of mind. And freedom from guilt.

Guilt is the gremlin of today. It is guilt that paralyzes a man's performance, undermines his self-confidence, destroys his motivation, headlines his weakness, and generally makes him a victim of the battered-man syndrome.

The good news is that peace of mind, God's kind, dissolves guilt in a forgiveness that leaves a man clean. It is David finding again the "right spirit" that he had lost when he sinned. It is the woman, any woman, hearing the words of Jesus, "Neither do I condemn thee." It is Peter, after he had denied his Lord, his proud heart caught and melted and changed by the forgiving smile of the Saviour. It is the crippled man, carried into the presence of Jesus, hearing those coveted words, "Son, thy sins be forgiven thee."

That, friend, is peace of mind. The *past* in the hands of a loving God.

And then, peace of mind is security. The *future* in God's hands. And who in this bewildering hour doesn't need it!

That is the tragedy of this grim generation. It feels it has no future. Today—college. Tomorrow—rotting in the jungles of somebody's war. Or crowded and polluted and sonic-boomed into oblivion. Is it difficult to understand the mania for "now"? How could it be otherwise?

But the youth of today *does* have a future. God has not been caught unprepared. The future is in His steady hands. There are no emergencies with God, no impossible situations, no personal problems too difficult for Him to solve or too small for Him to notice.

Peace of mind is not only the absence of guilt, the purging of remorse, the quieting of condemnation by the cleansing power of forgiveness, the sweeping clean of the past. It is a settled confidence in what God will do for you, for me, in the future. It is Isaiah saying, "Thou wilt keep him in perfect peace, whose mind is stayed on thee." It is Job saying, "Though he slay me, yet will I trust in him." It is Abraham saying to Isaac, "God will provide himself a lamb for a burnt offering." It is King Darius saying to Daniel, "Thy God whom thou servest continually, he will deliver thee." It is Esther declaring, "So will I go in unto the king, . . . and if I perish, I perish."

That is peace of mind!

Someone is saying, "Pastor Vandeman, you've been talking straight to me. Guilty—insecure. No one ever needed peace of mind more than I. But tell me. How can I find it?"

To make it very, very simple, here are three short, crisp statements that you and I need to make personally—and mean every word:

I am a sinner.

I can't do it.

But God can.

First, *I am a sinner.* There is nothing more difficult for a proud heart than to acknowledge—not weakness, not a personality problem, but *sin.*

It isn't popular to talk about sin anymore. It is easier to say a man is ill. It is easier, and some think kinder, to look upon a man, even a criminal, as simply the inevitable product of his heredity and environment, of his chromosomes and glands and body chemistry. Isn't it absurd, they say, to declare that a man has any moral responsibility for what he does?

Freud once declared that God was guilty of a careless piece of work when He made the conscience. Everywhere Freud saw the ravaging effects of guilt, you see, and he didn't understand. He tried to heal the fever by throwing away the thermometer. He often declared that a man cannot get well if his mind is constantly poisoned by a religious message that stresses his evil nature.

But that is exactly what God stresses—stresses because a recognition of need must come before the cure. He says, "The heart is deceitful above all things, and desperately wicked." Jeremiah 17:9.

Have we been blaming religion for our fears and our conscience for our guilt? Have we been making God the scapegoat for our emotional wounds and our psychic scars? God places the blame right where it belongs when He says, "All have sinned." Romans 3:23.

He calls every man a sinner—and evidently with good reason. There is no such thing as peace of mind until we come to that place where we say, "I'm to blame. No one else is responsible. God help me!"

And now the second painful fact: *I can't do it.* I can't manufacture peace of mind. I can't buy it in a bottle—or discover it in any formula. I can't generate it—or earn it—or deserve it—or obtain it by any penance, any sacrifice, any bargain with God.

When I think of bargaining with God, or trying to, I think of my friend Bill Barron. His outstanding musical talent has contributed to some of our It Is Written programs.

Bill was brought up a Christian. That is, he was taught, he was trained. But somehow it didn't take, and he grew up confused, unsatisfied, wanting Christ in his life but not willing to pay the price.

He joined the navy. And at last, one day aboard ship, the time had come. He couldn't put it off any longer. And he devised a rather unusual way of forcing himself to make a decision.

Down in a film locker of the ship he spotted a huge boxlike trunk. He asked a friend to lock him in that trunk for forty-five minutes. He reasoned that it was large enough that there would be oxygen enough for that long. And that ought to be long enough to work out his problem.

His friend said, "You've got to be kidding!"

And Bill said, "No. I mean it. Lock me in it!"

And what happened? Well, the first thing that happened was that his friend promptly walked away and forgot him for three and a half hours.

Bill tells me that the first hour he bargained with God. He said, "Lord, I'll do this for You if You'll do that for me." The second hour, he says, his bargaining wasn't quite so sharp. And the third hour there was no bargaining at all. And he found peace of mind.

Yes, after three hours and a half his friend suddenly remembered and came back on the double with the key.

But Bill was a different man. He had found peace of mind in one difficult step—*surrender!*

There is no other way. You don't have to be locked in a trunk. But you can't bargain with God for peace of mind. You can't buy it. You can only accept it. Jesus said, "My peace I *give* unto you." John 14:27.

There is no other way to get it—except as a gift, as a miracle of God's grace. Every human attempt to tame the tiger within, to quiet the conscience, to free the personality, will mean only disappointment. There is no peace of mind to the defeated man. No outward calm can ever cover his mocking heart. Peace is a gift. And peace is a miracle.

I am a sinner. I can't do it. And then No. 3. *But God can!*

25

A friend of mine tells of building a mysterious machine with his Erector set when he was but a small boy. It was bristling with springs and gears. This was to be no ordinary machine, he told his little sister. It would actually create life.

Unfortunately, she asked him how it worked. He wasn't prepared for that. But then he thought of an answer. He told her that he was depending on prayer—that he would pray hard, and God would work a miracle.

"Then what are all the gears for?" she wanted to know.

Why all the gears? Why all the springs? Why all the formulas? Why all the sidestepping of moral responsibility—all the shunting of blame? A man will never find peace of mind until he throws aside all his disappointing crutches and says, "Lord, I am a sinner. I've made a mess out of my life. I can't manage it. I bring my defeated life to You just as a child brings a stubborn toy to his father. You make it work. I can't. *But You can!"*

Someone is saying, "You speak of peace of mind in one difficult step. And I begin to understand. But I have always thought that there were really many steps—many things that we must do."

Yes. A man must acknowledge himself a sinner. He must repent. He must confess his sins and turn away from them. He must give up some things. And Jesus says, "If you love Me, keep My commandments."

But you see, all this is accomplished, all this is set in motion, in one act of surrender. "God be merciful to me a sinner!" All the rest comes naturally. It's all there—in one simple act of surrender. *Then the miracle takes place.* And you don't have to wait very long.

Dr. Paul Tournier, famed Swiss psychiatrist, orphaned early in life, in his study years became quite attached to a Greek professor who took an interest in him. Though not a religious man, the professor was kind.

Many years later Dr. Tournier, long after becoming a

Christian, completed his first book manuscript and wanted someone to read it critically. He thought of his old Greek professor.

The professor asked him to read aloud the first chapter. When it was completed, Dr. Tournier looked up for some critical reaction. The older man said merely, "Paul, continue." He read another chapter. "Paul, continue." He read the third chapter. Then the teacher said quietly, "Paul, we must pray together."

They knelt to pray. But Dr. Tournier could scarcely repress his surprise at this unexpected reaction. As they rose, he exclaimed, "But I didn't know you were a Christian!"

"Oh, yes, I am."

"But when did you become a Christian?"

"Just now."

Just now. That's how long it takes.

Chapter 3

Sand in the Machinery

A grain of sand in the wheel track of a bulldozer is no problem. But a grain of sand in the delicate mechanism of a lunar rocket—well, I wouldn't want to be a passenger!

Still more delicate, still more complex—in fact, the most intricately fashioned mechanism in the universe, so far as we know—is man himself.

Did you know that a neuron—just an ordinary nerve cell—is really a minicomputer, where something like two hundred communication paths may meet, and where messages are received and sorted and stored and then relayed as needed? And in your head there are no less than ten thousand million of these tiny computers!

What happens if a little bit of grit—some kind of mental or emotional grit—gets into the works? Trouble. Blown fuses. Short circuits. Tangled emotional wires. Usually the machinery doesn't grind to a jolting halt. But sometimes the situation created by crippled emotions is such that you wish it would!

A likely culprit is *guilt*. Guilt, more often than not, is the sand in the machinery of the emotions and the mind—and the body. Guilt is what is hugging this generation. The most persistent enemy of man's inner peace, the most difficult to eradicate, the one that refuses to be bypassed or ignored or explained away, is *guilt*.

A number of years ago, in a little German town, a woman found a basket on her doorstep one morning. In the basket were a pigeon and a note. The note demanded that she fasten a certain amount of money to the clip on the pigeon's leg and release it immediately—unless she wanted her house burned down that night.

She notified the police, and they acted fast. First they chartered two planes. Then they tied a streaming ribbon to the bird's neck and released it, instructing the two pilots to follow.

The bird rose into the air and wheeled around several times before taking a straight course. The people in the town watched the strange gyrations of the planes—and feared for their church steeple. Then the bird took a direct course, with the planes in pursuit and the police following in a fast car.

Soon the pigeon flew down to a loft. One pilot photographed the spot. The other contacted the police. The police rushed to the house and discovered two brothers hurriedly untying the telltale ribbon from the bird's neck. And of course they were arrested.

"But it just flew into our loft," they said. "It is not our bird."

The officers knew well enough how to test that story. They sent someone to release the bird again from some distance away. Again it just *happened* to fly back to the same loft. A second time. And a third. And then, of course, the men confessed.

Friend, do you identify with that story? Have you ever been caught in the act and forced to confess your guilt? I don't mean by the officers, by the law. Perhaps not even by family or friends. But by the repeated accusation of that inner voice we call conscience—until you have been forced to cry out in some moment when only God could hear, "I am guilty."

It is in the mind, in the emotions, you see, that guilt does its deadly work. And then it spreads to the body, leaving a man sick and defeated.

You have only to look around you, in your own circle of family and friends and work associates, to see a huge crowd of wounded and distressed men and women who are crushed by hidden guilt. That guilt may be real or imagined, definite or vague, recognized or unrecognized. But it is there.

And guilt can be absolutely lethal to the human personality. There is nothing in this world so destructive to inner peace as the sense of guilt. In fact, one writer remarks that "guilt as virulent as in the days of the medieval torture chambers has put modern psychology in business."

It isn't fear of the bomb that pays the rent for today's physicians of the mind. It isn't fear of communism. It isn't fear of air pollution or overpopulation or a Wall Street crash. Or even fear that California will slip into the sea.

No. These rarely make the list. And when they do, they are not the real problems. It is guilt, I say, that is bugging this generation.

But you see, try as he may, no physician, no student of the mind, can really deal effectively with guilt—except as he points a man to the cross. He may expose an old wound. But he cannot heal it. He may show you that your trouble is a long-buried sin. But he cannot forgive it. And forgiveness is what a man needs. Nothing less will do.

I never tire of reading the story of the man who was brought to Jesus on a stretcher. Jesus was teaching in a house, you recall, but it was impossible to get through the crowd. So the sick man's friends tore up the roof and let him down directly in front of the Healer.

Isn't it interesting that Jesus responded to all this urgency and determination and evident faith, not by immediately healing the man, but rather by first forgiving his sins? Listen: "Jesus seeing their faith said unto the sick of the palsy; Son, be of good cheer; thy sins be forgiven thee." Matthew 9:2.

Forgiveness. Was that what he had come for? Could it be that the man's illness may have been a result of his sin? Could it be that forgiveness was what he really wanted—more than healing?

Could it be that the divine Healer may have been watching the man's deep repentance—watching as his friends slowly made their way with their patient along the dusty roads— watching as he urged his friends to tear away the roof, anything that he might reach the One who could forgive his sins?

"Son, . . . thy sins be forgiven thee." See the stricken man lying there upon his stretcher now—relaxed, perfectly content, forgiven. Did physical healing even matter now? Were the words of Jesus that followed—"take up thy bed, and go"—just an extra bonus?

I think so. One thing is certain. Jesus understood that guilt and disease often go together. And He demonstrated that guilt can be healed.

But guilt, to be healed, must first be recognized. And modern man would rather do anything than to recognize it. We try to deny it, bypass it, ignore it, suppress it, explain it away.

Caught in the act—by an inner voice. And how does a man react? How should a man react? Let me take you back to the experience of two men who were very human, very much like us, and see how they reacted to being caught in the act, to the condemning voices that in their cases were very, very real.

The first is Saul, the man God had chosen to be Israel's first king. What a character this Saul! A man who was often in conflict with what God really wanted of him.

On this occasion God gave Saul specific instructions. The Amalekites, because their cup of rebellion was full and overflowing, because God had given them every chance, must be destroyed—every man, woman, child, and beast.

But Saul had ideas of his own. Those were good animals, prize stock. Why not bring them back alive from the battle—and then offer them as sacrifices? God would like that. And of course it would save their own animals that otherwise would have to be sacrificed. That was only good reasoning, good business.

And then why kill the king of the Amalekites? Wouldn't it be a better idea to bring him back a captive? Make him watch his own animals being sacrificed to the God of Israel. God should really like that!

The battle was over. And then the prophet Samuel appeared. And Saul greeted him with the words, "I have performed the commandment of the Lord." But Samuel said, in that embarrassing way that a prophet can have, "What meaneth then this bleating of the sheep in mine ears, and the lowing of the oxen which I hear?"

Caught in the act. But Saul was ready with an answer. The people. The people had done it. Somebody else. Not Saul. And they saved the animals for sacrifices. Don't You like that, God?

But God had an answer for Saul. "Hath the Lord as great delight in burnt offerings and sacrifices, as in obeying the voice of the Lord? Behold, to obey is better than sacrifice, and to hearken than the fat of rams." And there was more. "Because thou hast rejected the word of the Lord, he hath also rejected thee from being king." 1 Samuel 15:22, 23.

The finger of guilt had pointed. But Saul tried to bend the finger, tried to point it to somebody else. Is it any wonder that Saul's story was over? Oh, he went on being king for a while, until he took his own life. But it was Saul's reaction to God, Saul's reaction to the condemning finger of guilt, that really ended it all.

The story of David was very different. David was just as human. But watch.

David looked down from the roof of his palace one day. And there was the beautiful Bathsheba—bathing. You know the story. He brought her to the palace, and sent her home. And then you remember his sorry attempt to cover his sin by calling Bathsheba's husband, one of his trusted military leaders, home from the war. Repeatedly he tried to encourage Uriah to spend a little time at home.

But it didn't work.

David was desperate. And you remember what he did. He wrote a letter to Joab, his commander-in-chief, and sent it sealed by Uriah. The letter said, "Set ye Uriah in the forefront of the hottest battle, and retire ye from him, that he may be smitten, and die." 2 Samuel 11:15.

What a sin! And only David—and Joab—knew.

But God knew. And God sent the prophet Nathan to David. And Nathan didn't say a word about adultery—or murder. He simply told David a story. It was a story about a rich man who had large herds and flocks—and a poor man who had only one lamb, a family pet.

The rich man had a visitor. And instead of taking an animal from his own flock, he sent and took the poor man's one lamb and cooked it for his guest.

David's anger was white-hot. He thundered, "As the Lord liveth, the man that hath done this thing shall surely die!"

And Nathan looked straight into David's eyes for a long, silent, terrible moment. And he said, *"David, you are the man!"*

I try to imagine those moments. I think Nathan in sympathy looked away. He had said enough. And besides, David was his friend. He didn't want to make the hurt any greater. The truth was cutting deep.

Finally, in an agonized voice, the words came—six simple, unadorned, unqualified words: "I have sinned against the

Lord." No shunting of blame. No trying to bend the accusing finger to make it point somewhere else.

In those six simple words there is nothing of the fighter that he was, nothing of the great warrior, nothing of the proud monarch. They come from the broken soul of a man who has sinned.

David, unwittingly, in his response to the story Nathan told, had pronounced his own sentence. The man must die. Did this mean good-bye to the kingdom, good-bye to life itself? But one thing worried him even more. Did this mean good-bye to God? This was something between David and his God.

What did God do? He forgave him. He never does anything else when a man freely confesses his guilt.

And so Nathan leaves the palace. And now watch. What does David do now that the prophet has gone? Does he call in his public relations men? Get a statement out for the press. A denial. A clarification. Does he dictate a letter to Nathan—to put an official explanation down in writing? Does he get the family of Uriah on the phone? Or call Bathsheba in to tell her that the baby must die?

No. David is writing. Writing to his God. You can read his words, in all their deep pathos, in the fifty-first Psalm:

"Have mercy . . . wash me . . . cleanse me . . . I acknowledge my transgressions . . . against thee, thee only, have I sinned . . . purge me . . . wash me . . . hide thy face from my sins . . . create in me a clean heart, O God . . . cast me not away."

This is the man that God forgave. And He will do the same for you.

Guilt, you see, does not have to destroy. Guilt can provoke a passionate quest for a cure. Guilt can take you by the hand and lead you to God.

Chapter 4

More Than Spectacles

A man came into the outpatient department of a university hospital with an unsightly malignant ulcer on one temple. It had eaten through the skin and the muscle, and now it was sloughing out the bone. It was about an inch and a half in diameter. The inevitable and imminent prospect was a horrible death.

But all he had come for was a new pair of spectacles!

What a tragedy to be so confused about one's real need! Looking for spectacles when an ulcer is eating away the life! As if the spectacles of philosophy and culture and polish and rationalization could heal!

But you find no such confusion in the Scriptures. The divine finger is placed squarely on man's need. "The heart is deceitful above all things, and desperately wicked." Jeremiah 17:9.

If any one thing is clear in the Scriptures, it is this. There are only two camps. You are either for God or against God. Friends or foes. Like a lot of modern electronic gear, only on or off. Nothing in between. Forgiven—or not forgiven.

I like the way John Hercus says it: "If you meet people who argue that a good middle-of-the-road compromise is the ideal answer to a problem, if you hear anyone say that true peace is a sort of half-and-half between rebellion and obedience, if it is suggested to you that reconciliation of truth with error is the ultimate in human wisdom, then you can be altogether certain that you are not listening to the truth as it is recorded in the Bible!"

Even when we sincerely turn to religion, it is so easy to confuse information with a change of heart, knowledge with performance. Knowing about God, about the Bible, about the power of Christianity in the lives of men, isn't enough. Just to know the identity of the Healer doesn't heal. Knowledge and performance are two different things.

But when we start working on the performance part of it, we are still confused about who does what. Often we think we can accomplish by our own effort what can be achieved only by a miracle of God.

God says, "A new heart . . . will I give you." That is His answer. But we try to get by with patching it up. Like Pharisees in overalls, we try to do the work ourselves with the hope of presenting our Boy Scout merits at the gate of heaven.

God puts His finger, I say, on the real need. *We need a new heart.*

There is something about the resurrection that helps me understand what God really wants to do for us. We are all intrigued by the prophet Ezekiel's picture of a valley of dry bones. One moment a ghastly place full of skeletons, all the flesh gone, the bones bleached white in the glare of the sun. And then they begin to rattle, to move, to join together. They are knit by tendons, clothed with flesh. They live. What a picture of what God plans to do!

Then come down through the centuries to the days when Jesus walked with men. More than once He demonstrated His power to call the dead to life. There was the widow's son, and the daughter of Jairus, and Lazarus. What incredible demonstrations of resurrection power!

And yet—even these fall short of what God intends to do for us one day. These three lived again—but still with mortal bodies. They still had to pass under the power of death.

The story of our risen Lord—that is the resurrection story of all history! Watch Him as He walks for miles and miles on feet that had had nails wrenched out of them thirty-six hours before. It takes more than X-rays and orthopedic surgeons to explain the risen Lord. Here was resurrection at its best. Here was a prototype of what God intends to do for us.

Translate it then, though words are inadequate, into what God wants to do with our hearts. A new heart. This is resurrection, too. Not cardiac massage. Not a heart stimulated to run a little longer. Not a heart with a valve replaced. Not a heart with the infection of sin arrested but not removed. Not a heart dependent on some miracle of electronics to keep it going. Said the prophet, "A new heart also will I give you, and a new spirit will I put within you: and I will take away the stony heart out of your flesh, and I will give you an heart of flesh." Ezekiel 36:26.

What a promise! Never a sickness without a remedy. Never a sin without a Saviour. Never defeat without the promise of victory.

We move now to the last book of the Bible, where the Great Physician tells us clearly about our need. Listen to these plain words:

"Because thou sayest, I am rich, and increased with goods, and have need of nothing; and knowest not that thou art wretched, and miserable, and poor, and blind, and naked." Revelation 3:17.

Straight diagnosis. Honest diagnosis. Evidently there is something about sin that blinds us to our true condition. The deeper we go into it, the more we cannot see its nature. We think we are all right—needing just a pair of spectacles perhaps—when an ulcer numbers our days.

These straight words were addressed to Laodicea, one of the early churches, a type of the church in our day.

It has been my privilege to travel across Turkey, the land of the seven churches, the land where past and present are married in sand and stone and clay. And there in Western Anatolia, above the banks of the meandering Meander River, where peasants still turn up ruins as they plow, is the site of Laodicea.

This was once a thriving center of the wool and cloth industry. Today its ruins are a lonely, desolate sight. Laodicea, producer of rich fabrics, yet, according to the Revelation, needing to be clothed.

I was intrigued with the report that a document has been found, written in the name of the town itself, which says boastfully, "I am famous. I am wealthy. I lack nothing."

Is it any wonder that the prophet used Laodicea to represent this self-satisfied, self-sufficient generation? Wretched, miserable, poor, blind, naked. But not knowing it.

But God never makes a diagnosis without offering a prescription. Listen: "I counsel thee to buy of me gold tried in the fire, that thou mayest be rich; and white raiment, that thou mayest be clothed, and that the shame of thy nakedness do not appear; and anoint thine eyes with eyesalve, that thou mayest see." Verse 18.

Not spectacles, but eyesalve from the pharmacy of heaven. Not glitter, not wealth, not fame, not material possessions, not things—but the gold of faith and love. Not culture and polish and veneer, but white raiment—the character of God reflected in you and me.

That is the prescription. And heaven's pharmacy is never closed!

Chapter 5

Taproots

In Hertfordshire, in the heart of old England, was a garden dominated by a weeping willow tree. Characteristically its branches drooped in a giant circle, and the sharp-tipped leaves gave to the tree the appearance of finely spun lace.

The children of the family played under this tree as they grew up, its branches falling round them like a tent. At first to their surprise, and later to their disgust, they noticed that every year long, ugly shoots with large round leaves would grow out from the trunk. Aspen leaves they were, so unlike the delicate, arrow-shaped willow leaves.

This was puzzling. Aspen leaves on a willow tree? How could such a thing happen? The mystery was solved when the old gardener explained that a weeping willow shoot had long ago been grafted into an aspen tree. In time the willow had overcome the aspen, until all the branches were willow. Yet each springtime aspen leaves would grow out from the trunk. The children would indignantly pull them off. Had they been left, they would have spoiled the whole appearance of the lacy tree.

In this weeping willow with its aspen leaves we see a parable of life. And is it any wonder that we find the most accurate parables of life in nature? For the God of nature, the God who made the tree, is the God who made the soul. And the laws that govern the growth of all living things are the laws of the Creator, who implants new life in your heart at the time of conversion and watches over its growth.

Trees and souls! Parables are sometimes very, very real—as real in this case as a strange and unexpected paradox of the Christian life that every man and woman needs to understand.

You see, there is a tendency with some to expect all conflict to end at conversion. It seems only natural to assume that when the life is given to God, all inner contention should give way to unruffled peace.

For a few days, or weeks, or months, this may seem to be the case. There is new power within, new strength to overcome weakness, and a sense of forgiveness that makes a man radiantly happy in his new faith.

Thank God that such an experience may be permanent, and sometimes is. But often this is not the case. Strange things may begin to happen. Old temptations, old feelings, old thoughts, may clamor again for recognition. A man may yield momentarily to these old impulses. He may find himself suddenly irritable and bad-tempered. And he thought he could never be that way again!

The personality is troubled. The new Christian is surprised and ashamed at the appearance of the telltale shoots of the old life. He tries to pull off the "aspen leaves" so that no one else will know. But he is divided inside. He knows that a house divided against itself cannot stand. And he is discouraged.

Said Spinoza, the Dutch philosopher, "Do not weep. Do not wax indignant. Understand."

And whatever Spinoza may or may not have known about the Christian life, who can say that his words do not fit the need of the man who discovers this strange division within himself? Weeping will not help. Growing angry will help less. Understanding the problem will do wonders!

Now it is most natural to experience a rapid climb to new heights through the miracle of conversion. But many are unprepared for the tableland that sometimes follows—a tableland of victory interspersed with occasional defeat. They think that conversion promises uninterrupted victory. And when it doesn't happen, their disappointment is overwhelming.

In fact, it is just this baffling mystery of inner conflict and division when peace and harmony have been expected that leads some to ask, "Why does life seem to glide along so smoothly for the man who has made no profession of following his Lord and who cares little about the spiritual life? Why are there no apparent conflicts within him? Yet on the other hand, the man who has been born again and calls himself a Christian seems to be opposed at every turn. Why is this?"

The answer is quite simple, and very evident as we think it through. The man without Christ has only one nature, the nature with which he was born. There is therefore nothing to oppose it. But the man who has accepted Christ, who has submitted to the miracle of conversion, has had new life grafted into his soul.

Two natures, you see. Like the willow and the aspen. The one nature is his by right of physical birth. The other is his by right of spiritual birth. And these two are antagonistic. That is why there may be struggle in the life of the Christian, at least at first, and why there may be no apparent struggle in the life of the non-Christian.

The implanting of new life within a man at the time of conversion may set up certain tensions within the personality. These are described by the Apostle Paul: "For the flesh lusteth against the Spirit, and the Spirit against the flesh: and these are contrary the one to the other: so that ye cannot do the things that ye would." Galatians 5:17.

I like the way Dr. Phillips translates these lines: "For the whole energy of the lower nature is set against the Spirit, while the whole power of the Spirit is contrary to the lower nature. Here is the conflict, and that is why you are not free to do what you want to do."

Evidently this is why the Christian is faced with a conflict within, while the non-Christian seems to drift along with no evidence of struggle. So fundamental is the change conversion brings, that the vitality of the new life will probably set up a disturbance within.

The Christian, then, is not always ushered into unruffled calm. A settled conviction, to be sure. But a new nature now contends with the old. Even the Apostle Paul faced the problem of contending with the remnants of the old nature. It was long after he had first experienced the power of the indwelling Christ, long after he had entered into a life of consistent victory, that he wrote, "I die daily." 1 Corinthians 15:31.

Every day the claims of Christ conflicted at some point with inclination. Every day he found it necessary to crucify the old nature. He said, "I keep under my body, and bring it into subjection: lest that by any means, when I have preached to others, I myself should be a castaway." 1 Corinthians 9:27.

This is not theory. This is not a fictitious conflict. It is as real as today. There are now two natures within the soul. *One of them will rule.*

Shall we make it practical? Tomorrow morning as you arise fresh to meet a new day, ask yourself the question, "Which of these two natures will control my life during the waking hours of this day?"

I would like to tell you now the answer to that question.

But someone says, "Pastor Vandeman, you don't know me. How could you tell which nature will rule in my life?"

True, I may not know you personally. But I do know this: *Whichever nature is the stronger will rule your life tomorrow.* If the spiritual nature is the stronger, it will rule your life tomorrow. If the old nature is the stronger, it will rule your life tomorrow.

And may I go as far as to say that whichever nature rules you determines your destiny? For when our Lord returns to earth, when He descends through the blazing heavens, your standing in that day will depend upon which nature then rules your life. And it will be one or the other. It cannot be both.

But now please notice the secret. Whichever nature you *feed* will be the stronger. By a divine act the Creator has implanted new life and power in your soul. God has done in you a work of grace beyond the ability of man to bestow. But now comes your part. You can either feed or starve that new nature. The outcome of the conflict, in a very real sense, then, depends on you. The essential thing now is to utterly neglect that which feeds the old nature, while turning your attention to feeding the new life within. Remember, the nature you feed will be the stronger. And what feeds one starves the other.

Do you see now why so many—and their number is legion—live on in a state of frustration? The problem is simple. They have been feeding both natures just enough to keep them alive. They have just enough of Christ in the life to produce conflict, and not enough to produce control.

It was Moses who said, "Be sure your sin will find you out." And Jesus said, "By their fruits ye shall know them." If ever those words apply, they apply here. For the man or woman who compromises just a little, thinking no one will ever know, will sooner or later be surprised and embarrassed to see those telltale shoots of the old life appearing when least expected.

The whole problem is easily solved. Then why continue to live in conflict? Why perpetuate a civil war inside when the secret of growing peace and inner power is so simple?

Let me put it this way: Shall we suppose that two ferocious

animals are fighting each other. The outcome of the battle is anyone's guess. But then suppose that for some reason the fight is interrupted and one of the animals is starved for a few weeks and then allowed to limp weakly back into the conflict again. What will be the outcome of the battle now? Which one will win? Is there any question? No. The one that has been fed will win.

Feed the new nature, friend. That is the priceless secret of growing, satisfying peace.

But you ask, "How do you feed the new nature? How can I be sure that it is strong enough to control my life?"

The health habits of the soul arc not unlike those of the human body. *Let it breathe. Feed it. Let it grow strong by exercise.*

Prayer is the channel for the life-giving oxygen that penetrates the lifeblood of the new nature. Let the soul *breathe.* Pray not as a duty, not merely when you are in trouble. But talk to God as you would to a friend. Tell Him your needs, your desires, your joys. Let it be the spontaneous, unrehearsed outpouring of the soul.

I could write many pages about the rules of prayer. But I would rather say this: God is more interested in you than in the rules. If at first you do not know the rules, if you happen to come in the wrong door, God will not send you back to come in again the right way. Pray—and know the joy of it!

And then *feed* the new nature. God's Word invites you. Every page is nourishing food. You have talked to God. Now let Him talk to you—through the open Book. You will find the promises of Scriptures like leaves from the tree of life that hang over heaven's wall to this fallen world. And remember, "Man shall not live by bread alone, but by every word that proceedeth out of the mouth of God."

And finally, the deepest desire of the newly healed heart of course, is to bring others to the same Source of healing. Such service is the *exercise* of the soul.

A doctor once found a little dog with a broken leg. He took the little fellow home, put the leg in splints, and kept him until he was well. But as soon as the dog was able to run about the house, he disappeared. "That's gratitude," thought the physician. "As long as he needed me, he stayed. As soon as he didn't need me, he ran away."

Then next day there was a scratching at the back door, and there was the little dog. But another little dog was with him. *And that other little dog was lame!*

The secret cannot be kept. It has to be shared!

Prayer—Bible study—sharing. These open the floodgates. These make it possible for the strength of the living Christ to flow unchecked into your life. Keep the floodgates open.

Yes, whichever nature is fed will be the stronger. And when you take hold of that simple, practical truth, you will be surprised at the problems it will solve.

Every day we live, we face a series of choices. The clothes we wear, the books we read, the company we keep. The thoughts we think, the care we give our bodies, the food we give our minds. How we spend our recreation time. All these must enter into Christian living, for all these affect the health of the soul. We need consecrated minds and hands and feet these days.

Which nature does it feed? Here is the question that will settle many problems of right and wrong. It will be amazing how this simple formula will clear up even minor questions that seem inconsequential in themselves. Which nature does it feed? That will settle it.

But now, which nature have *you* been feeding? Has compromise within brought defeat, failure, discouragement? Have you been feeding the old nature and starving the new—or feeding the new just enough to keep it alive?

Trees and souls are not unlike. The Japanese have a way of stunting forest trees so that they never grow higher than potted plants. They cut the taproot, the main feeders, so that the trees live only on the small surface roots. Destined to be forest giants—but stunted, dwarfed, their taproots cut!

Your life can be stunted, tied by compromise and sin, frustrated in its purpose, dwarfed in its destiny. Or it can be like the giant redwood—free, unshackled, rooted in the centuries, and lifting its head to God!

Cut loose, friend! Come clean with God. Sink your roots deep in the strength of the mighty One. And live!

Chapter 6

Running the Gauntlet

In the pioneer days of early America settlers often had to face the attacks of Indians who resented their presence. When these befeathered warriors had taken a man captive, they would sometimes take delight in playing with their victim as a cat with a mouse. For instance, a captive might be told that he had a chance for life if he could safely pass between two long lines of his enemies armed to the teeth with tomahawks and knives. This, of course, meant almost certain death. But on rare occasions a man might escape by running like a streak of lightning or dodging like a rabbit.

This was called *running the gauntlet,* an expression used ever since. And however cruel and heartless the old Indian practice, it was little different from the array of satanic weapons today. Men and women and youth are still running the gauntlet. It is a run no less hazardous. And the mind is the theater of action.

The forces of evil were never so strong, so subtle, and yet so attractive. And it is no use thinking that the fight is going to be anything but fierce and furious. It was the Apostle Paul who said, "Put on all the armour which God provides, so that you may be able to stand firm against the devices of the devil. For our fight is not against human foes, but against cosmic powers, against the authorities and potentates of this dark world, against the superhuman forces of evil in the heavens." Ephesians 6:11, 12, N.E.B.

Someone may be saying, "You don't know what I'm up against, or you would understand why I can't be a Christian. If I were in a job like yours, it would be easy. But in that shop I am surrounded every day by a crowd of men whose talk is unprintable and whose lives are little better. How can you expect a fellow in circumstances like mine to be a Christian?"

Surprising as it may seem, victory in the titanic struggle for the soul depends not on our own strength or determination to resist, not on our speed or ability to dodge the knives of the enemy, but upon which power is in control of the fortress of the mind.

You see, when a man begins to serve Christ, the enemy of God does not relax his attentions. Rather, he intensifies his attack. With diabolical cunning he prepares his ambush. It may be a surprise attack when a frontal attack is unlikely to succeed. It may be an attack so cleverly camouflaged that it is difficult to recognize its source. And always the strategy is changing, carefully calculated to catch a man off guard.

I can tell you this. The devil is angry. He knows his time is short. His deceptions, his attacks, his temptations, in a day like this, are not going to be crude and clumsy. Rather, they are going to be subtle, clever, shrewdly adapted to the day in which we live—and to your particular weaknesses.

The target is the mind. Because that means the conscience. That means the will. And that means the destiny.

And so the enemy determines to steam up the mind and dim its windows—because if he can conquer the mind, he can conquer us. That is where the real battles are fought, and won or lost. He will capture the mind in any way he can. He will use alcohol. He will use drugs. He will use hypnotism.

But remember that any breaching of the mind, any deliberate weakening of it, any control of it by another—even temporarily and for seemingly worthy purposes—can sabotage the soul's defenses without your knowing it. To lightly surrender that citadel of the soul to a human being, for however commendable a reason, may hold devastating consequences.

Just a caution. But think it through. That caution may save your life—and your soul!

The mind can be a fortress well guarded—a fortress that Christ holds in a revolted world. Or it can be weak, undefended, vulnerable to attack. It is no wonder that God says, "Keep thy heart with all diligence; for out of it are the issues of life." Proverbs 4:23.

What is this *heart* that we are to guard so diligently? Is it the organ that pumps blood through the arteries? No. It must be something central, deep within the springs of life. Can it be anything less than the mind? The mind—the *heart* spoken of in the Scriptures—is the seat of the affections, the center of conscious reasoning, the citadel of the soul.

You remember that Jesus said, "For from within, out of the heart of men, proceed evil thoughts, adulteries, fornications, murders." Mark 7:21. Do these proceed from anything but the mind? And Paul describes the Word of God as "a discerner of the thoughts and intents of the heart." Hebrews 4:12. The mind alone is the source of thoughts and intentions.

Yes, as we come to grips with the real issues in this battle between Christ and Satan, between good and evil, it is evident that transformation of the mind is absolutely essential. The heart, the mind, needs to be changed. Nothing less will do. And such a change is not only necessary but possible, for Paul says, "Be not conformed to this world: but be ye transformed by the renewing of your mind." Romans 12:2.

Remember the promise, "A new heart also will I give you."

And renewing it does need, for "the heart is deceitful above all things, and desperately wicked."

I have been delighted and amazed at how clearly the Scriptures—long before the birth of modern psychology—present the central problem. For instance, the ancient Job had never heard of the subconscious mind when he asked, "Who can bring a clean thing out of an unclean?" and when he answered, "Not one." Job 14:4.

Deep in the subconscious mind of every one of us lie inclinations and agelong leanings—filth that rises to rest like scum on the surface of the mind.

The question that long haunted me was this: Could conversion affect the subconscious mind? If not, what hope is there for anyone?

But, thank God, it does! The Scriptures clearly indicate it. The stroke of Omnipotence can sink to the depths and sweeten and purify the whole. The mind—even the subconscious mind—can be changed by the power of God.

This brings us face to face with a very familiar word—*temptation*. Surprising as it may seem, temptation is not sin. Temptation is with us at all times. As long as we have body and brain, temptation will attempt to reach us through both. We carry it with us like germs.

But the fact that we are tempted need not be a guilty secret. Temptation itself is not sin. I repeat this because the very suggestion of wrong seems to bring pollution with it. If we mistakenly believe that temptation is sin, we will blame ourselves for suggestions of evil even while we detest them. This will bring a sense of condemnation and discouragement which, if continued in, ends at last in actual sin. We fall often from the very fear of having fallen.

The enemy stands ready to make the best of any situation. He brings the suggestion of evil and then turns around and says, "How sinful you must be to have such a thought! You must not be converted! You must not have the real thing!"

And we drop to our knees and ask forgiveness for the devil's sins. It is as though a burglar should break into your home and then turn and accuse you of being the thief.

You see, the point is that the enemy can never overcome a man until he has the cooperation of the man himself. He may gain that cooperation by trickery. He will gain it in any way he can. But there is no sin until by thought, word, or deed we encourage the tempter. Temptations may allure. They may perplex and harass and distress. They may create an atmosphere in which it is hard to breathe. But they cannot contaminate without an act of your will. They cannot triumph over you without your consent. It takes two to make a successful temptation.

Would the familiar switchboard illustration help us here to understand this very real distinction? Shall we say that in the switchboard of every heart there are two main trunk lines— good and evil, right and wrong, Christ's line and the devil's line? But no matter how frequent or insistent or excited the flash of the enemy's light, it cannot contaminate unless you make contact. You need not answer the light. The light is the temptation. Answering it is the sin.

One more word about temptation. It can leave you stronger. Every time you are tempted, you either rise or fall, you either conquer or are conquered. Your reaction to temptation can leave you better—or worse. If you trust in the power of Christ and are victorious, you are stronger and better prepared for the next attack. If you trust to your own strength and lose, you are weaker, more vulnerable, less able to withstand the next onslaught. And only those who have met temptation in the strength of the mighty One will stand in the last crisis.

Personally, I know of no greater help in overcoming temptation than the words of Jesus, " 'But courage! The victory is mine; I have conquered the world.' " John 16:33, N.E.B.

When I got hold of the idea that I would never meet a sin or a temptation that He had not already conquered, it became a tower of strength. For why did I, with His power at my command, need to surrender to that which had already been conquered?

I think of the legend of the ancient warrior who during a battle had his head cut off. But so involved was he in fighting that he fought on and killed many, until a woman cried out, "Your head is gone. You are dead." *So he fell down and died.*

Evil fights on its brainless battle. But why permit it to bully you? Its head is gone.

One of the easiest things in the world is to develop an inferiority complex before sin. We yield to the feeling that sin is a permanent part of things, that it cannot be eradicated, that our case is peculiar and different, that because God loves us He will overlook our faults—or a hundred and one other excuses. Therefore we are defeated in the mind at the very start of the battle. And never forget that every battle of the soul is fought, and won or lost, in the mind—before your family or your friends know anything about it.

When a strong temptation comes your way, why not try asking it to bend its head? And there on its neck you will see branded the figure of a cross—the mark of its losing encounter with the Conqueror of Calvary. Why surrender? By God's grace you can win. You are on the winning side. Confidence can lead to victory—not confidence in yourself, but confidence in the Saviour who has already conquered. His victory can be yours.

I hope this point is clear enough to encourage you to try its secret. It is where our attention is centered that counts. Constantly looking to ourselves will bring only weakness and defeat, for we see nothing but our own inadequacy and failure. When we look to our interior states and feelings, we discover a very unrepresentative self, a very defeated self, instead of Christ.

You see, sin thrives on attention, even negative attention. Self would rather be thought badly of, remember, than not be thought of at all. And whatever gets the mind, gets you. Whatever invades the mind, invades the fortress of the soul.

Even a sincere attempt to fight sin in the mind can lead to succumbing to it. The Lord has a better way. He asks us to change our minds by looking to Him. Here is our central human need. For more tired, discouraged, defeated minds result from frantic attempts to fight sin in the emotions, to expel it, than from any other experience that comes to the Christian. Is not God's way better? Simply turn your attention elsewhere.

I keep remembering the Indian fakir who came to a village declaring he would demonstrate how to make gold. The villagers gathered around as he poured water into a huge caldron, put some coloring matter into it, and began to repeat magic words as he stirred.

When their attention was temporarily diverted, he let some gold nuggets slip down into the water. Stirring a little more, he finally poured off the water, and there was the gold at the bottom of the caldron. The villagers' eyes bulged. The moneylender offered five hundred rupees for the formula, and the fakir sold it to him. "But," the fakir explained, "you must not think of the red-faced monkey as you stir. If you do, the gold will never come."

The moneylender promised *to remember that he was to forget.* But try as hard as he might, the red-faced monkey sat on the edge of his mind, spoiling all his gold!

Just so, to try to forget your sins will only drive them into your consciousness. To forget them, *center your attention elsewhere.*

No true healing of body and mind and soul can come from within ourselves, from any inherent powers that we may possess. It must come from God. To be sure, we can cooperate with the laws of God as they operate within that fantastic instrument called the human mind. But such healing and transformation as the human heart longs to know can come only with the lift of the implanted power of God.

I think of the building of a giant bridge across a portion of New York's harbor. Engineers were searching for a base upon which to rest one of the mighty buttresses. But they discovered, deep in the mud and practically buried, an old sunken barge full of bricks and stones. It had to be moved. Yet in spite of every device it remained firmly held to its muddy bed.

At last one of the engineers conceived an idea. He gathered other barges about and secured them by long chains to the sunken wreck *while the tide was low.* Then all waited. The tide was coming in. Higher and higher rose the water, and with it the floating barges. Then creaking and straining on the chains, that old boat was lifted from its viselike grip—raised by the lift of the Atlantic Ocean!

Need I draw a parallel?

I ask you, Is your mind like an old barge full of bricks and stones, gripped by memories you long to forget, held by agelong leanings and habits you would give anything to be released from, bound by fears and unholy imaginations? Has every human device failed to break the power of their viselike grip in your life? Just know that the lift of the mighty God will deliver you. He is able. But you must choose.

The enemy of God and man is not willing that this priceless secret be clearly understood. For he knows that when you receive it fully, his power will be broken. And you will be free!

Chapter 7

It Happened in a Penitentiary

It was a sparsely settled West in those days—and sometimes as wild as its reputation. Cities and towns were scattered. Gun slaying was frequent. Often he was safest who was fastest with the trigger.

Into this setting walked a man known as Harry Orchard, though that was not his real name.

Harry Orchard was doubtless the most notorious criminal of his generation. His name was linked with the desperate class struggle and the attending lawlessness that marked its history in our great Northwest around the turn of the century. Theodore Roosevelt was President. And Frank Steunenberg was the newly retired governor of Idaho.

Harry Orchard was accustomed to being a fugitive from justice—alone, unhappy, desperate. He had made money fast and spent it faster until, deep in debt, he found himself open to the appeal of corrupted labor forces. Soon he was in the inner circle—actually planning organized crime.

Inscribed on his gun were twenty notches. It was for those notches that he was being hunted. But now he faced his last gruesome assignment—taking the life of Frank Steunenberg.

Governor Steunenberg was a man of great force of character, fearless and able. He had been utterly oblivious to any personal danger in his fight to control the lawless elements in his state—though his life had more than once been threatened.

Mrs. Steunenberg, his devoted wife, was a lovable Christian character, determined that her children should be taught in the ways of the Lord. Her husband, however, though a great statesman, made no profession of Christianity.

One morning late in 1906 Mrs. Steunenberg was conducting family worship in an upstairs room. Her husband had joined them, as he frequently did. Often, in his clear tenor voice, he had joined in their songs.

On this morning her heart was particularly burdened. Unable to cover her concern, she appealed to him, especially in view of the repeated threats against his life, the constant dangers he faced, to give his heart to the Lord and place himself under divine protection.

He did not answer. But she could see that his mind was agitated, that God was speaking to his heart. He paced the floor in evident struggle. Then he ended the silence by breaking into song. The song he chose? "Nearer, My God, to Thee."

Perhaps that was his answer. Evidently some decision had been made. For later that day, unknown to his wife, he told some of his friends that his life was going to be different, that from now on he wouldn't be doing some of the things he had been accustomed to do.

Little did he know how short a time was his. For Harry Orchard had already constructed the fatal bomb. As Frank Steunenberg returned to his home that evening, he opened the gate that triggered the infernal device.

The end came within hours. The city was surrounded by state militia. The search was quick and thorough. Harry Orchard had carved the last notch on his gun.

The spotlight of national attention was upon the trial that followed. It was one of the great legal battles in American history. The famed Clarence Darrow and William Borah fought for long months over issues that involved the future of the labor movements in North America.

In the center of it all, of course, was Harry Orchard. About to be convicted? Yes. But also, through a surprising set of circumstances, about to be changed. That is our story.

A doctor in Chicago, David Paulson, hearing of the trial, felt impressed to send Harry Orchard a Bible. When it arrived, the prisoner at first refused to accept it. Of what use was a Bible to a man like him? A Bible and a twenty-notch gun were not exactly compatible.

But something was bothering him. Since his apprehension the words had been ringing in his mind, "No murderer can be saved." He didn't know the source of those words. But might they be from Scripture? Were they in this Book? He decided to find out.

Of course he didn't find those words. Nowhere does the Bible say that a murderer cannot be saved. Rather, what Harry Orchard found in the Book was a Saviour who says, "Him that cometh to me I will in no wise cast out." John 6:37.

And then something else happened. One day as he was waiting for court proceedings to begin, the warden approached him. "Orchard," he said, "Mrs. Steunenberg's son wants to see you."

Immediately the boy entered, trembling before his father's assassin. He held out a package and said in a frightened voice, "Mother sends you this."

But now it was Harry Orchard's turn to tremble. What sort of revenge was this? What would the wife of his victim be sending him? A bomb?

He nervously opened the package and found, to his relief, only a book. Then he realized that the boy was still standing there.

"Mother says that she forgives you the terrible wrong that you have done our family. She asks you to give your heart to Christ. She says her only hope is that you will be saved in God's kingdom."

Imagine, if you can, the thoughts of that hardened mind. To think that the wife of the man he had so heartlessly murdered would send him not a bomb, but forgiveness! If Christianity could do that for a woman who had been so wronged, it must be something very, very real. And whatever the book was, he would read it.

Actually it was a little book called *Steps to Christ*—probably the finest book ever written, outside the Scriptures, about the *how* of Christian living. Not one of you should be without it.

He read the book eagerly. And he continued to read his Bible. And Mrs. Steunenberg herself visited him a number of times. Everywhere he was finding not condemnation, but forgiveness. Everywhere except in court.

But the trial and its outcome now became less important than what was happening in Harry Orchard's own heart. Forgiveness—as he found it in the Book, and as he saw it demonstrated in a life—was doing its work. It all helped to bring a hopelessly confused man through the dark night of conflict—helped him to make the critical and all-important decision for God and for right. He knew now what he must do—and what he *would* do. He would confess to God to clear his own soul. And he would confess to the world to right as far as he could his terrible wrong to mankind.

His confession, he knew, would lay bare a long succession of crimes that would shock humanity. His sins seemed to reach down to hell and to mount up to heaven. "They were so terrible," he said, "that even if I bitterly repented, I had the dread fear that God would never forgive me. But there was still a tiny flickering ray of hope."

His conversion was genuine and deep. He prayed into the

long nights. He searched the Book. As his sins would tower above him like a forbidding mountain, he would fall again to his knees. Fellow prisoners thought he was losing his mind. No, he wasn't losing his mind. Rather, he was finding his God.

The plea now was *guilty*. But before the God of heaven this prisoner stood forgiven. Already he was free. He welcomed the sentence—life imprisonment—for it was not release from prison that he craved. He simply wanted to live to share with others the freedom of soul that he had found.

Years later, many years later, he was to say to me, "I well remember the day I walked into this penitentiary. As the jailer turned the key in my cell, I felt instinctively that I would never be a free man again. That was more than four decades ago. I am still incarcerated within that prison. But in spite of these years of confinement, I have . . . a freedom of soul that I never knew once in the days when I was physically at liberty. Stone walls and metal bars have held my body captive, but my soul has long been free."

That was the freedom he wanted to share—even in the early days of his incarceration.

And what was happening? Something more than forgiveness. Something more than an inner freedom. Living contact with the Lord Jesus Christ began to change that man. The lines in his face began to soften. It was now an honest face. God's grace was doing its work.

Right here I would like to introduce something that may seem like a diversion. But I think you will see that it is very much to the point.

Sooner or later every Christian comes in contact with two words that may seem a little hard to understand—*justification* and *sanctification*. They may seem like stuffy theological terms. But in them we find a very wonderful truth.

Justification, you see, has to do with forgiveness, with a man's standing before God. When a man is forgiven, his standing is completely changed. He is accepted before God just as if he had never sinned. No longer does God consider him guilty.

But isn't he still guilty? True, his past life has not changed. Even God cannot change the past. But He does something very wonderful about it. He takes the perfect record of the life of Jesus—and calls that record ours. He credits it to our account. He covers our sins with the perfect righteousness of His Son. When He looks at us, He doesn't see the miserable mess we have made of things. He sees the perfect life of Jesus.

How amazing! All eternity won't be long enough to understand the wonder of forgiveness. And it all takes place in a moment of time.

But forgiveness is not all. If the gospel of Christ can offer only forgiveness, if we are condemned to go right on sinning, what hope is there? Only a life of alternate sin and forgiveness. But if the power of Christ can forgive us, but never change us, there is something wrong. The gospel is lacking where we need it most.

But thank God, *the cross can do more about sin than forgive it!* It can change a man. And that is where sanctification comes in. Sanctification has to do not with *calling* a man good, but with *making* him good; not with *counting* him righteous, but with *making* him righteous. Justification credits the life of Jesus to his account, but sanctification puts the life of Jesus into the man. One changes a man's status. The other changes the man. One forgives him for breaking the law. The other puts the law into his heart. One gives him a title to heaven. The other makes him fit for heaven.

I think you can see that while justification takes only a moment, sanctification is the work of a lifetime.

I know of no finer illustration of justification and sanctification than was demonstrated in Harry Orchard. You see, when he asked forgiveness, immediately his standing with

God was changed. But his face was still that of a hardened criminal. Whatever God did with his heart, with his mind, at that moment, whatever miracle took place, he still had the background, the leanings, the appearance, of a criminal. He was a criminal—*forgiven*.

His standing changed. But now the whole man was being transformed. And an interesting circumstance, it so happened, demonstrates just how great the change was. The judge who found him guilty, who had observed him so closely all those months of the trial, took a year's leave from the bench immediately after the trial. A year later he returned. His first case was that of an accomplice of Harry Orchard, and of course Orchard was called as a witness.

The judge called for Harry Orchard to be brought in. He was escorted to the stand. But the judge said, "This is not Harry Orchard! This is not the man I tried!" He could not believe that the kind, honest, noble face before him was that of the hardened man who sat through those months in his court.

Think of it! The change in one short year!

Yes, God did more for Harry Orchard than to forgive him. It was not just his status that was changed. The man himself was changed.

Could this change be what Paul meant when he said in 2 Corinthians 5:17, "If any man be in Christ, he is a new creature: old things are passed away; behold, all things are become new"? Evidently.

Certainly the change in Harry Orchard could not be credited to culture or environment or self-discipline. No, like Nicodemus of old, he had met his Lord in the night. He had heard Him say, "You must be born again." And he may never have understood it. But he had experienced it. He was a new man. And he was free!

It may be difficult for a generation brought up on test tubes and slide rules, electronics and jet propulsion—I say, it may be difficult for some to understand the working of one of the surest laws in all the universe: "Ye shall know the truth, and the truth shall make you free." John 8:32.

Remember the words of Harry Orchard after forty years of imprisonment? "Stone walls and metal bars have held my body captive, but my soul has long been free." It sounds like Lovelace's familiar old seventeenth-century hymn:

> "Stone walls do not a prison make,
> Nor iron bars a cage."

Someone is saying, "I'd give anything to know just one day of freedom and peace like that."

Friend, it can be yours—not just for a day, but from this moment on. All that God did for Harry Orchard, He wants to do for you. Here is the promise—brief, pointed, powerful: "For sin shall not have dominion over you: for ye are not under the law, but under grace." Romans 6:14.

That is real freedom. Think of it! Sin—the world's heaviest burden. Sin—the root of guilt. Sin—the basis for fear, unrest, and frustration. Sin—the cause of separation from God. Sin—the cruel, relentless slave master. Sin need not have dominion over you. Sin need no longer hold you in its power. Why? Because the grace of God can give you power to stop sinning.

I shall never forget the day that I talked with that eighty-three-year-old saint in the Idaho State Penitentiary. A saint in overalls, with a rugged, sun-tanned, swarthy face. But peace, freedom from sin and guilt, shone in every line of Harry Orchard's face as that dear man told me the intimate details of the story I have just related. I was seeing through misty eyes, I must confess. For I was seeing God's amazing grace, His living power, His measureless love—in action.

It was on another prison wall, I am told, that some unidentified prisoner had scrawled these words:

"Could we with ink the ocean fill,
And were the skies of parchment made;
Were every stalk on earth a quill,
And every man a scribe by trade;
To write the love of God above
Would drain the ocean dry;
Nor could the scroll contain the whole,
Though stretched from sky to sky."

Measureless. Enduring. Strong. Greater than all the world's need. And best of all, it's for sinners! It's for you! It's for me!

Chapter 8

"To Your Knees, Sir!"

An inexperienced climber was making his way up one of the mountains in the Swiss Alps. It was a steep, hazardous ascent. But he felt secure in the company of two stalwart guides.

At last, breathless, after several hours of strenuous climbing, they reached for those rocks protruding through the snow above them—the summit.

Wishing to let the young stranger have the first glorious view of heaven and earth, the guide ahead stepped aside to let him go first.

In his excitement, the young man forgot his caution. He forgot the stiff gale that was blowing across the summit rocks. Wishing to get a better view, he leaped to his feet.

But instantly the chief guide dragged him down as he shouted, "To your knees, sir! You are never safe here except on your knees!"

You and I have climbed almost to the summit of human history. We can almost look across into eternity. Just a few more time-splintered rocks, and it will all be over.

Nuclear gales are threatening to break loose over our heads.

Our air is already tainted. Fulfilling prophecy is about to converge in one final drama of glory and destruction.

To your knees, sir! No other position is safe in this hour! But it seems to be contrary to man's nature to get down on his knees.

Oh, we're willing to stand proudly as the colors go by. Willing to stand at attention as the drums beat and the sturdy anthem rises. Willing to stand when somebody offers the invocation. Willing to show respect. But to get down on our knees would be to admit our need. And it's contrary to our nature to say, "I need help."

A modern perversion of psychology has taught us too well that everything we need is within the human personality. We don't need anything outside of ourselves. All that is necessary is to develop the spark of divinity that sleeps in every man. We don't need God. We are little gods ourselves. These are the subtle, or not so subtle, suggestions that are thrust into our thinking.

We are so self-sufficient, I say. We don't need forgiveness anymore. Just take Brand X. Minutes after taking it the man you shouted at in the shop is your friend again, your little girl loves you as much as before you scolded her so mercilessly for driving her tricycle into the flower beds. Neighbors have made up, and the boss forgets he was going to fire his secretary. It's all in a little pill. We don't need forgiveness. We don't need God. So it seems.

It is to this self-satisfied, self-sufficient generation that God says, "To your knees, sir!"

Someone is saying, "But I don't know how to pray. Tell me how to pray so that my prayers will be answered."

Let us turn to the Bible, for there is no better lesson in how to pray than the story Jesus told: "Two men went up into the temple to pray; the one a Pharisee, and the other a publican. The Pharisee stood and prayed thus with himself,

God, I thank thee, that I am not as other men are, extortioners, unjust, adulterers, or even as this publican. I fast twice in the week, I give tithes of all that I possess. And the publican, standing afar off, would not lift up so much as his eyes unto heaven, but smote upon his breast, saying, God be merciful to me a sinner." Luke 18:10-13.

You get the picture. One is saying, "God is surely lucky to have me." The other is saying, "I need God." And you know which prayer was answered!

Here then is the clue. The secret of answered prayer is a matter of attitude. A condition of heart. "Lord, help me."

But how shall we begin? What does God promise, and how can we receive it? What can you expect God to do for you personally, and under what conditions?

Let us turn first to one of the most striking promises Jesus ever made regarding prayer: "Again I say unto you, That if two of you shall agree on earth as touching any thing that they shall ask, it shall be done for them of my Father which is in heaven." Matthew 18:19.

Now this is just one of a number of breathtaking statements that Jesus made about prayer. He also said, "And all things, whatsoever ye shall ask in prayer, believing, ye shall receive." Matthew 21:22. "If ye shall ask any thing in my name, I will do it." John 14:14.

There seems to be no ceiling, no limit, to what is here promised. And let me say this: The honor of God's throne stands behind every word.

But just here someone interrupts. "But, Pastor Vandeman, if all the universe runs on unalterable law, then how can prayer really change anything? Doesn't that make a miracle impossible?"

Yes, the universe does operate on fixed laws. And we can be glad it does. If fire burned today but didn't burn tomorrow, if water boiled at one temperature today but froze at the same temperature tomorrow, we would have an intolerable situation. We would not be able to survive. Life is possible only because of these unchanging laws.

But before we conclude that these fixed laws cancel out our prayers, we should remember that laws interact with other laws. Iron will not float—but mighty ships sail the oceans. Aluminum will not hang in the air—but our jets streak through the skies. Does a plane break the law of gravity? No. But there are laws of aerodynamics as well. And these laws interact.

Isn't it possible that the Creator may have at His disposal many laws, both physical and spiritual, of which we know nothing? Yes. There is nothing wrong with the promises, breathtaking as they may be. The God who made them knows how to fulfill them.

And yet some have eagerly, in faith, taken the promises of our Lord to their knees and come away disappointed, frustrated, not knowing why their expectations were not realized.

Why? What is wrong? Isn't faith enough?

To be sure, faith is essential. "Without faith it is impossible to please him: for he that cometh to God must believe that he is, and that he is a rewarder of them that diligently seek him." Hebrews 11:6.

But suppose we think it through. Jesus said, "If two of you shall agree, . . . it shall be done." Does this really mean what some have thought? Do you really believe that God would pledge Himself to grant *anything* that two or three people agree to ask, regardless of how unreasonable their request? Here we have two people praying for rain. And over here are two people praying that it will not rain. And God caught in the middle!

No. God has not committed Himself to be governed by the whims of men. What chaos we would have!

The Greek word that is translated "agree" means literally "to symphonize." Picture a symphony orchestra, its players tuning their instruments. What is the object of all this careful adjusting of pitch? Is it that groups of two, here and there, shall be in tune with each other? Or is it that the individual players shall be in tune not only with each other but with the master pitch? And of course you see the point. In our prayers we need to be in tune, in agreement, not only with each other but with God. So the promise is not quite as simple as it seemed.

And then Jesus said, "If ye shall ask any thing in my name, I will do it." Could it be that there is more involved in praying in His name than simply attaching it to the end of our prayers? I think so.

Evidently if prayer is to be answered, it must be in harmony with the will of God. It must be in tune with what the Creator knows to be best. "And this is the confidence that we have in him, that, if we ask any thing according to his will, he heareth us: and if we know that he hear us, whatsoever we ask, we know that we have the petitions that we desired of him." 1 John 5:14, 15.

Some things, of course, we know are in line with His will. If a man prays sincerely for forgiveness of sin, he can know that his request is immediately granted. But in some areas we may not be so sure. We must leave it to Him.

Our prayers must be according to His will. And they must be *reasonable*. But does that adjective really fit some of our prayers—and some of our ideas about prayer? and some of our motives?

Do we think of prayer as some sort of fire escape—an emergency exit to be used only when other doors are blocked? Do we call on God in trouble—and forget Him in the sunshine? Do we invite Him into only those situations that we can't manage nicely ourselves? Do we pray only when we want something? A little boy remarked, "I didn't pray last night because I didn't want anything."

Do we ask for health so that we can waste it away again? Do we get ourselves into trouble and then expect God to get us out so that we won't be embarrassed? You remember the little girl who prayed, "Lord, please make Boston the capital of Vermont, because I said so on my examination paper."

Prayer is communication—communication with God. But we human beings seem to be adept at finding ways to short-circuit that communication. And rebellion in our lives, of course, completely breaks the contact. "Your iniquities have separated between you and your God, and your sins have hid his face from you, that he will not hear." Isaiah 59:2.

Disturbingly clear, isn't it?

And now we come face to face with one of the most difficult words in the Christian vocabulary—*surrender.* There can be no real faith, no real touching of the throne of God, without surrender.

We need to learn to pray what Catherine Marshall has called the prayer of relinquishment. We need to come to the place where we say, "All right, Lord, I give up. Whatever You decide is all right with me."

But we are so human. We tell God precisely how to answer our prayers. And then, if He doesn't follow our instructions, we are tempted to reach out to stay His hand.

I say, you may be tempted to do that. But don't, friend. Don't!

> "Don't touch His hand!
> A Master Artist paints.
> What you have thought to do
> Would only blur the picture
> That He makes.
>
> "You cannot see
> That which His mind intends

To make of you.
Your awkward touch might easily
Upset the colors, and the easel, too.

"Don't touch what He is doing.
You fear that He might spoil it all
Unless you hold Him back.

"But wait!
Don't touch His hand!
For He is God—
    And He is wise—
        And He is love!"

Yes, wait. You can trust a God like that!

It's a priceless revelation to discover that God knows best how to answer prayer.

I wonder if you have heard the parable of the three trees that lived in the forest long ago. John Ellis Large tells it in his book *Think on These Things*. Listen:

"The first tree prayed that, when it was hewn down, it might become part of the timbers of a noble palace, the most magnificent building ever shaped by the creative hands of men. . . . Instead, it was faced with the bitter fact that its lovely grain was being used to throw a rude stable together. But it was the stable in which the Christ Child was born!

"The second tree petitioned God that, when the axe should be laid to its roots, its planks might be fashioned into the hull of the lordliest vessel that ever sailed the seven seas. . . . Instead, when it was chopped down, it was used to form the hull of a lowly fishing vessel; and the tree resented the insult to its grandeur. But that insignificant schooner was the one from which Jesus preached His incomparable words at the edge of the little Sea of Galilee!

"The third tree beseeched God that it might never feel the bite of the cruel axe, but that it might go on for years pointing its proud finger toward the sky. . . . Instead, the dark day came when the woodsmen arrived and laid the sharp blade to its resisting roots; and it cried out against God with every blow. But the shaken tree was fated to become the crossarms and the upright of the Cross of Calvary, destined to point its noble finger toward the sky forever!

"Not a single one of those trees lived to see its fondest wish come true. Not a single one got its deepest prayer answered, nor its own will fulfilled. But God, in fulfilling *His* will for those three trees, granted them a fulfillment infinitely beyond anything they could have desired or hoped for!"

You can trust a God like that. Can't you, friend?

Chapter 9

Risk

Pizarro and his small party of adventurers were stranded on the shore of South America and nearly given up for lost. At last a boat from Panama came to rescue them. But Pizarro refused rescue.

Instead, with his sword, he drew a line in the sand and said to his men, "South of this line lies hunger, storm, and death. North of it lies pleasure and ease. But south lies Peru with riches. North, Panama and poverty. For my part I choose south!"

Eighteen men stepped across that line with Pizarro, ready to take the risk.

Yes, there is a risk in every challenge. But those who are willing to draw lines in the sand and stand for their convictions, those who are willing to give hours without count, devotion without recognition, will find gold.

Did you know that even the man who bends his knee takes a risk? For he who prays sincerely is inviting divine invasion of the soul. He is participating in an encounter with the Creator that will change all his future life. He will never be the same again.

For instance, it may seem a simple thing to pray, as did David, "Create in me a clean heart, O God; and renew a right spirit within me." Psalm 51:10.

A simple prayer, I say. But what if a man doesn't want to be clean? What if he isn't willing to part with his bitterness and his pride?

And did you realize that you may be taking a chance when you turn the pages of a book? Of course, there are some books you can read with no agitation, no disturbance, no troubling of the waters. But not so with some. And not so with the Bible. You can't read very far without finding an appeal for commitment. You can't read very far without encountering claims that you cannot ignore.

That is why some have read eagerly for a time, drinking in its refreshing truth. And then they have laid it down because they knew that if they read one more page their lives would be changed. And they weren't sure they wanted to be changed!

You see, there is a risk in searching for truth.

At this very moment there are thousands of eyes turned wistfully toward heaven, asking that God will lead them into truth. And that prayer will be answered. God has promised that it will. "And ye shall know the truth, and the truth shall make you free." John 8:32.

You will know the truth. The truth will make you free. But what if you don't want to be free? What if you don't really want to be set free from that habit that binds you? What if you don't want freedom—yet?

Any man who is willing to follow truth will find it. But it will cost him something. Said Jesus, "Think not that I am come to send peace on earth: I came not to send peace, but a sword. For I am come to set a man at variance against his father, and the daughter against her mother, and the daughter in law against her mother in law. And a man's foes shall be they of his own household." Matthew 10:34-36.

Yes, truth will cost you something.

A pastor had just presented challenging truth to his evening audience. As the last hymn was being sung, he slipped out the side door. He wanted to make his way quickly to the front of the church, where he could greet the people as they left.

In the meantime, a young businessman present at the meeting, deeply convicted by the truth he had heard, and disturbed by its newness and its claims, had also slipped out of the church and stood thoughtfully in the shadows. They almost collided. He took the pastor by the lapels of his coat and exclaimed with deep concern, *"Pastor, all my life I have prayed for truth. But I never thought to ask God how much it would cost!"*

Yes, truth can be disquieting, for suddenly we discover that the price is high. It means being changed. It means being disturbed. It means being involved. And some don't *want* to be changed. They don't *want* to be disturbed. They don't *want* to be involved.

A man makes his way home at night, his newspaper under his arm. Suddenly he sees flames. A neighbor's house is on fire. He stops to watch. A crowd gathers. Property is endangered. Children are trapped inside. Conscience speaks.

But he says, "Why should I get my hands dirty? I'm comfortable. I'm dry." And so he stands by. He watches. A half hour later he looks up from his newspaper to remark to his wife about the spectacular blaze he saw just down the street on the way home.

He has his reward. He is clean and comfortable and dry. But his comfort has already condemned him, and his clean hands have damned him.

You say it couldn't happen? No. You might have said it a decade ago. But not today. The story of Kitty Genovese and the thirty-eight silent witnesses to her stabbing has multiplied on the nation's conscience in city after city.

A telephone receptionist was beaten and threatened with a

razor. Breaking away from her assailant, she fled down a stairway screaming, "Help me! Help me!" About twenty people were attracted by her screams. She fell down the last steps to the landing. The crowd grew to forty. Not one person moved to help.

Robbers had poured lighter fluid over their bound victim and set him afire. "Sure, I heard screams," said the neighbor in the next apartment. "In fact, they were so loud that I had to turn up the volume of my television set."

Two policemen were injured in an automobile accident near a drive-in. Customers jeered when carhops rushed to their aid. "Let them die—who cares?" commented one onlooker.

Do we need to go on? Doesn't anybody care? Are we nearing the time when one neighbor will greet another, "Oh, was that *you* screaming?"

Yes, more and more, people don't want to be involved. They don't want to be questioned. They don't want to be called into court. They want to stay comfortable. But their comfort condemns them. More and more people are haunted by the memory of nightmares they watched from their windows and did nothing about. "Samaritans are very scarce these days," says one reporter.

How can we explain this calloused cowardice, this immunity to challenge, that is so typical of our generation? How can we defend this grotesque paralysis of conscience that is creeping upon all humanity?

Men and women are saying, "Don't tamper with me. Don't invade my privacy. Don't disturb me."

Could this be why so many are hesitant about commitment to Christ? They don't want to be involved. They seem to sense a risk in following Jesus. And they say, "Why should I follow Him? Why should I become involved? Why should I take the risk? I'm comfortable. I'm relaxed. Why make a commitment?"

Afraid to be involved? Afraid to take the risk?

Friend, there is risk at the very heart of Christian commitment. And it is inescapable. Said Jesus, "He that taketh not his cross, and followeth after me is not worthy of me. He that findeth his life shall lose it: and he that loseth his life for my sake shall find it." Matthew 10:38, 39.

The most frightening word in the Christian vocabulary is the word *surrender*. How do you spell it? Most people I know spell it with four letters—*r-i-s-k*.

We fear it because we do not know what it may mean. We fear it because we do not want to let go the management of our lives. We fear it because God may ask us to give up something we do not want to give up.

A few years ago, in old Jerusalem, I stood at the spot where it is said that Abraham and Isaac learned what surrender meant.

You remember the story. Life was moving along very satisfactorily for Abraham. God had at last given him the promised son, and that son was growing into manhood.

Then suddenly came that strange but unmistakable request from God. Abraham was to offer sacrifice upon a distant mountain. And that sacrifice was to be his son!

Picture it if you can. Abraham is crushed and dazed. But he does not delay. With Isaac at his side, he starts out in the early morning. Preparations are made. They carry with them the wood for the fire.

Together they journey in silence. How can he tell his son? How can he answer the question he is sure to ask?

At last they near the summit. And Isaac breaks the silence. "My father," he says, "behold the fire and the wood: but where is the lamb for a burnt offering?"

What a question! Abraham answers, his voice faltering, "God will provide himself a lamb." His words are part faith and part postponement. For he knows that at the top of that mountain he will have to say to the son he so dearly loves, "You are the lamb!"

Imagine the stark drama of that summit scene. And think of the faith of the young man Isaac. How easy it would be, in the strength of early manhood, to overcome his aging father and escape. But, no. He is willing to enter into this act of surrender along with his father.

Finally the knife is raised. The moment has come. If we were watching from a secluded spot nearby, we might call out, "Be careful, Abraham! Aren't you taking too big a risk? After all, Isaac is the son given you by a miracle. Abraham, aren't you carrying your religion a little too far?"

We would call it risk. God calls it faith.

And then—you know the outcome. The knife is raised. But an angel stays his hand. Abraham has said that God would provide a sacrifice. And now God does. A ram caught in a thicket is offered instead of his son.

Wiping the sweat from our brow, we exclaim, "What a risk he took!"

We say there is a risk in surrender. It is this that frightens us. It is this that holds us back. It is this that keeps us from commitment.

Tell me. We agree that the risk in surrender is the problem. Obviously this is the block. But if I could prove to you, even though it may seem to contradict what I have already said—if I could prove to you that there is no risk at all in surrender, that the risk is only apparent, that it is not real, just a phantom, then would you follow your Lord, wherever He may be leading, without delay?

You see, Abraham had simply decided that God could have anything He wanted in his life. He wasn't taking chances. He wasn't daring anything, risking anything. He was just trusting a God he had come to know. He was convinced that a God who could give him Isaac by a miracle in the first place could raise him from the dead if necessary.

Isaac shared that faith. And in it he was perfectly safe. He was safer on the altar of sacrifice than he could have been in the halls of sin. In fact, Isaac was never safer than when he lay surrendered upon the altar, in the hands of a loving God. Abraham and Isaac risked nothing. But they gained an invaluable understanding of the plan of salvation.

There is no risk in surrender. God is not standing by with a list of unpleasant requirements ready to impose them upon us the moment we surrender. There is no risk in surrender—except when we do it halfway. It is the partial, cautious, soft-pedal commitment that brings problems.

Peter did it halfway. You remember how he longed to walk on the water. And Jesus said, "Come."

Now anyone knows that a man cannot walk on water. A man is no match for the turbulence that waits to swallow him.

But picture what happened. Peter hears the one word, "Come." He drops the oar and slips down over the side of the boat, gingerly touching the water. He takes a first cautious step, then another. Excitement, probably tinged with pride, rises within him. He—Simon Peter—is walking on the water! Are his companions watching?

For a moment he takes his eyes off Jesus. For a moment he takes back the management of his life—takes himself out of the hands of the Saviour. And he begins to sink. Humbly now, his pride soaking wet, he cries out, "Lord, save me!" His companions cannot help him. He cannot save himself. In Jesus alone is his hope.

I like these words from a pen I believe to be inspired: "It is safe to let go every earthly support, and take the hand of Him who lifted up and saved the sinking disciple on the stormy sea."

Safe to let go every earthly support!

Do you see? It's perfectly safe. Surrender is not giving God permission to release an assortment of troubles into our lives.

Surrender is just knowing that God loves us—and then acting accordingly. It's as simple as that!

Someone is saying, "I want to surrender. But I don't know how."

You say, "I cannot control my thoughts. I cannot control my feelings. My promises and my resolutions are like ropes of sand. What shall I do?"

Has it ever occurred to you that *decision is surrender?* God does not negotiate with your feelings and your emotions. What He wants is the decision. What He wants is the choice. What He wants is the will. He wants you. And the will is you.

Remember those four words. *The will is you.*

You find yourself caught in a maze of emotional contradiction. Desire pulls at your mind. Taste clamors for attention. Lust rears its ugly head. Fear torments you. reeling depresses you.

But *the will is you.* God does not decide your future on the basis of your feelings and your fears. He judges you not by inborn desires but by deliberate decision. *The decision is you.*

Let me illustrate. I have prayed with men who desperately wanted release from the habits of tobacco and liquor. And I have seen God instantly take away the craving. Thank God for miracles like that!

But for many the craving does not so quickly diminish. The craving is still there. But the will, the decision, is in control. They do not yield. And I say, Thank God for that kind of victory!

What does Heaven write into the record? The craving—or the victory? The desire—or the decision?

You know the answer. The desire is not the real you. *The will is you.*

We need to understand the true force of the will. It is true that we are weak in moral power. We cannot change our hearts. We cannot cast out the demons of sin that possess our minds.

But when you decide—when you cry out for a power out of and above yourself—the powers of the soul, strengthened with divine energy, will obey the dictates of your will. By yielding the will to God, you ally yourself with all the power of His throne. And it involves no risk.

It was God, you see, who took the risk. He took the risk when He created man with the power of choice. Someone might choose to sin. And someone did!

God took a risk again at Calvary. I say it reverently. Jesus took a terrible chance when He allowed Himself to be nailed to that cross. He could not see through the portals of the tomb. The sense of separation from His Father, the sense of His Father's displeasure with sin, was so keen that He feared the separation might be eternal. That is the chance He took.

You say there is a risk in following Him? You fear the cost? You fear the loneliness? You fear divine invasion of the soul? You fear the detachment, the isolation from the crowd, that it might involve?

But wait, friend. It is He who took the risk. It is He who stayed upon that cross when taunting voices cried, "Come down!"

Something deep within Him echoed, "Yes, come down! Why should You take the chance? Why should You risk Your life when eternity might never give it back?"

But, no. He took the risk!

And now, friend, we have talked frankly. Is it risk that has stood in your way? Yet we have discovered that the risk of surrender is only apparent. It is not real. We have been diverted, sidetracked, fooled by an illusion of danger, bullied by the unreal.

And so I ask you, If this is true, then what stands in the way of your complete commitment to our wonderful Lord and Saviour Jesus Christ?

Remember, it's perfectly safe!

Chapter 10

Conscience

Watchdog—guardian angel—tormentor of the soul! As elusive as your shadow—and just as persistent. It can be a comfortable companion. Or it can make a man turn pale at the lightning—or the rattle of a leaf. We call it *conscience!*

What is this mysterious extra sense in the soul of man? There have been scores of definitions—some philosophical, some abstract, some painfully practical. But simply said, conscience is that capacity within us that decides whether a thing is right or wrong and urges us to act accordingly.

It is the traffic light of the soul, if you please. It tells you when to go. It tells you when to stop. Or it may urge you to proceed with caution. Just as the traffic light is the signal for the laws that govern traffic, so conscience is the signal—the voice of direction—for God's moral law of the universe.

And conscience, like our five senses, functions through the mind. There must be a mind alert to interpret its direction.

You may remember the tragic account of the New Jersey train that plunged off an open drawbridge. It was the accident that couldn't happen—yet it did. That commuter train actually sped through three red lights and plunged off the open bridge into Newark Bay.

Why? The engineer had evidently suffered a heart attack. The signals were working, but there was no mind to interpret and act upon them. And for some reason that particular train had not been equipped with a dead man's switch.

Neither is conscience equipped with a dead man's switch! That is why the conscience cannot give adequate direction when the mental faculties are obstructed or impaired in any way. Or when we are unconscious. Or, unfortunately, if we are under the influence of alcohol or narcotics. Such artificial blocks effectively silence the conscience and lay open the sacred precincts of the human mind to the impressions of chance or evil.

No doubt you have heard the claim that conscience does continue to function during hypnosis. Unfortunately, this is not all the truth. Some of the most experienced authorities only smile at the claim that it is necessary for hypnotic suggestion to fit in with the subject's moral code. They tell us that, on the contrary, it is possible through deep hypnosis to force normally conscientious individuals even to commit crime.

You can see that this is completely logical. The hypnotist recognizes that he cannot expect a subject to carry out his suggestions while in full command of his reasoning faculty. Therefore, as one authority says, "the therapist must partially inactivate, temporarily, the center of conscious reason in the individual." He must silence the watchdog. And that is a dangerous practice!

No, it is simply not possible for the conscience to do its work under such conditions. The conscience cannot function normally without the conscious mind.

Suggestion, of course, is all right in its place. Every television commercial we hear is suggestion. But suggestion needs to go through the thinking machine. It needs to confront reason. It needs to be screened and censored and controlled by the conscience. The conscience must be working. And it cannot work without the mind.

Evidently there is something here that we need to understand.

Now the word *conscience* does not occur in the Old Testament. But from the beginning of the Bible record conscience is very much in evidence. Our first parents felt the emotions of shame and fear at wrongdoing. Cain complained that his punishment was more than he could bear. Joseph's sensitive conscience led him to meet temptation with the words, "How then can I do this great wickedness, and sin against God?" Genesis 39:9.

Listen to this quaint way of expressing David's deep conviction of sin: "And David's heart smote him." 2 Samuel 24:10. And Job, in his faraway day, determined, "My heart shall not reproach me so long as I live." Job 27:6.

Happy is the man today who vows to keep his conscience clean!

Someone is asking, "Is conscience the same as instinct?"

No. An animal is compelled by instinct to act in a certain way. It is by instinct that the birds fly south in winter. It is by instinct that they find their way over the trackless oceans and back again in spring. Not so with man. He is urged, but not compelled. He is free to choose—and then either to suffer or enjoy the consequences.

Then could it be that conscience is simply the result of accumulated experience and environment, and therefore subject to change from generation to generation?

We have just passed through a generation that thought so. True, a baby soon learns that things tipped over are broken. A man soon learns that if he does not leave home in time, he misses his train. A woman soon learns how to set her table if she is to be accepted socially.

But what such reasoning fails to take into consideration is that these things do not touch moral issues. They have little or nothing to do with conscience. Sin is more than personality deficiency, a mistake in judgment, or social maladjustment. The so-called conscience of this past generation answered to no higher authority than public opinion. No absolute standard was necessary, we were told. Standards were supposed to dwarf the personality. If a lad feels like breaking up the furniture, don't cripple his expression!

A famous psychologist once declared, "Damn the absolute creeds!" And the minor voices of that philosophy ever since have echoed that decree. Millions of intellects were twisted. Religious faith declined. Confusion set in in regards to guilt, forgiveness, and even prayer.

Then we began to reap. Our deepest problems today are simply the product of the past generation's twisted thinking.

We panic today as we see our streets and our campuses out of control. But what could we expect? When we silenced the voice of conscience in our boys and girls, we took away their guardian angel.

A frightening number of morally confused men and women are crowding the doors of our psychiatric clinics. But again, What could we expect? The idea that conscience is a creature of man's own making—that sin is only a built-up figment of morbid imagination, not something to turn from—is producing more conflict in modern minds than any other one thing.

Is it any wonder that millions of heartsick, bewildered men and women are seeking out an understanding counselor to whom they can talk—talk interminably about themselves? The talk itself is supposed to be healing, to bring composure. And sometimes it does, to a degree. But there is lasting help only if somewhere along the line the counselor, whoever he may be—psychiatrist, physician, or minister—can put down a ladder that will show a man how to get out of his mental and spiritual tangle.

And that ladder can tolerate no evasions, no bluffing, no acting as though nothing had happened. No attempt to heal the conscience by destroying it. Guilt must be lifted and the heart set singing through the forgiveness of God. There is no other way. The God who made the conscience tells us how to heal it.

"If we confess our sins, he is faithful and just to forgive us our sins, and to cleanse us from all unrighteousness." 1 John 1:9.

"Come now, and let us reason together, saith the Lord: though your sins be as scarlet, they shall be as white as snow; though they be red like crimson, they shall be as wool." Isaiah 1:18.

That's release, friend. Guilt can be redemptively met only by Calvary. The feelings of guilt must be laid at the cross, or they will poison the springs of life. Guilt can be pushed back into the subconscious and fester and make you literally sick. Or guilt, if you let it, can take you by the hand, place its burning finger on the need of your soul, and lead you to God.

The healing of the conscience and the healing of the body go hand in hand. Listen:

"There is no health in my limbs, thanks to my sins." Psalm 38:3, Moffatt.

"Confess your faults one to another, and pray one for another, that ye may be healed." James 5:16.

"Thy sins be forgiven thee. . . . Arise, and take up thy bed, and walk." Mark 2:9.

A soul that is torn and sick with a sense of guilt, a conscience weighed down with the burden of sin, can find permanent release and healing only with the assurance of forgiveness before God. There is no other way. There is no other ladder out of guilt.

But someone is asking, "Suppose I do accept the forgiveness of God. Then will my conscience be dependable and accurate from that time on?"

No, not necessarily. The conscience now is clean. Guilt has been removed. But your conscience must prow in moral sensitivity. It must be educated. Let me explain.

The conscience decides what is right and wrong. But it decides only on the basis of the information it has. It is not some sort of spiritual Geiger counter that peers into moral issues and decides them by some psychic power. Conscience simply prompts a man to act on what he believes to be right or wrong.

For instance, conscience will not reprove a man who picks up a glass of liquor believing it to be lemonade. When he finds out what it is, then conscience speaks. If a man had never heard of the effects of strong drink, conscience might not speak at all. Conscience must be educated.

Do you see the danger? It is here that we need a divine, infallible authority. Conscience can be trusted only when it is educated to speak in harmony, in unison, with the voice in the Book. In fact, all teaching that denies the supreme authority of God's Ten Commandments in the soul of man, denies the authority by which conscience, if it is to be accurate, must judge.

On the other hand, the more a Christian studies the Word of God, the more accurate his conscience will be. The more willingly he approaches its pages, the more often the voice within him will say distinctly, "This is the way, walk ye in it." Isaiah 30:21.

Some time ago I was visiting, with an attorney friend of mine, in the home of the ninety-four-year-old mother. As we studied the Word of God together, her pet parakeet came and perched on my shoulder. As I would let the Scriptures unfold a point of truth, the little bird would say, "That is so!" And then as another gem of truth appeared in all its clarity, again it would say, "That is so!"

I am not asking you to read anything unusual into this

incident. Just how or why that little mite said those words clearly that day, I do not know. He may have heard them said. But however that may be, what an illustration of the priceless approval that can be yours! As you peruse the inspired pages, the Holy Spirit, the One sent to guide you into all truth, will whisper into your heart the confident word of direction, "That is so!" And He will add, "This is the way, walk ye in it."

But—and this is important—the conscience can also be damaged. It is a delicate instrument. We dare not abuse it, or even neglect it, if we expect to profit by its warnings. The Apostle Paul in 1 Timothy 4:2 speaks of those whose conscience is "seared with a hot iron." Here is not a condition in which conscience is completely erased, but where conscience ceases to function in the normal way because its voice has been disregarded.

Which one of you has not tried out a new alarm clock that on the first morning startled you out of bed? But if you should turn it off and go back to sleep, and repeat the process day after day, you would soon sleep through its warning. The bell does not ring any less loudly. It is your relationship to the bell that is changed. Your consciousness develops a condition in which the bell can no longer be heard.

Just so, the Spirit of God can be grieved, His voice quenched, His moral alerts resisted—until at last there is silence. And unfortunately, a man may not know that a tragedy has occurred. For even that empty silence is misinterpreted by some.

Alexander MacLaren describes the process by which conscience becomes seared and hardened in words that have haunted me ever since I first read them: "An old historian says about the Roman armies that marched through a country, burning and destroying every living thing, 'They make it a solitude, and they call it peace.' And so do men with their consciences. They stifle them, sear them, forcibly silence them, somehow or other; and then, when there is a dread stillness in its heart, broken by no voice of either approbation or blame, but doleful, like the unnatural quiet of a deserted city, then they say it is peace."

God forbid it—in either your life or mine! For when a man has stilled the voice of warning, when he has stilled the only voice of God to his soul, what more can God do?

It is only a divinely guided conscience, a conscience as sensitive to right as the needle to the pole, that will give a man courage to stand for conviction though the heavens fall. No martyr ever went to the stake with a weak, vacillating, spineless conscience!

I think of that winter night when a Roman legion was encamped in a little lakeside town in France. There are many versions of the story. But evidently forty spiritual heroes, unwilling to renounce their faith, were sentenced to die out on the frozen lake. Banded together in the benumbing cold, they began to sing. The stern, proud commander, on watch from his comfortable tent, heard the words:

> "Forty wrestlers, wrestling for Thee,
>   O Christ,
>   Claim for Thee the victory
>   And ask from Thee the crown."

Strangely moved by this unusual testimony, that hardened soldier, so used to cursing and frantic pleas for mercy, listened intently. These were men of his own company, men who had angered the emperor by their faith. These were his forty heroes. Must they die?

He moved out into the cold, gathered driftwood from the shore, and built a huge fire with flames leaping high into the night. Perhaps this would lead them to renounce their faith and thus save their lives. But, no. Again the sound of the refrain met his ears, weaker now:

"Forty wrestlers, wrestling for Thee,
    O Christ,
    Claim for Thee the victory
    And ask from Thee the crown."

Then suddenly the song changed.

"Thirty-nine wrestlers, wrestling for Thee,
    O Christ—"

And all at once, as the song still floated in across the ice, one of the prisoners climbed up the bank and dropped by the fire, a huddled mass. The song of the forty was no more. One of the heroes had disavowed his faith.

On the shore, clearly outlined against the fire, stood the commander. Strange things were surging in his breast. Then suddenly his soldiers saw him take one brief look at the pitiful specimen before him and throw off his own cloak. Before they could stop him, he raced down the bank and across the ice to the freezing prisoners, casting back the words, "As I live, I'll have your place!"

In a few moments the song, with a fresh note of triumph, was wafted again to the soldiers who had gathered, fearful and awestruck, on the silent shore:

"Forty wrestlers, wrestling for Thee,
    O Christ,
    Claim for Thee the victory
    And ask from Thee the crown!"

It is only when the conscience speaks with such authority that such victory can be yours. And who knows how soon you will need it!